DESIGNING

WEB INTERFACES

TO ES

A

KR

S

American Library Association

Chicago and London 1999

While extensive effort has gone into ensuring the reliability
of information appearing in this book, the publisher makes
no warranty, express or implied, on the accuracy or reliability of the information, and does not assume and hereby
disclaims any liability to any person for any loss or damage
caused by errors or omissions in this publication.

Trademarked names appear in the text of this book. Rather
than identify or insert a trademark symbol at the appearance of each name, the author and the American Library
Association state that the names are used for editorial purposes exclusively, to the ultimate benefit of the owners of
the trademarks. There is absolutely no intention of infringe-
ment on the rights of the trademark owners.

Composition by the authors using Arial and Bookman Old
Style typefaces

Printed on 50-pound Victor Offset, a pH-neutral stock, and
bound in 10-point Bristol cover stock by Victor Graphics

The paper used in this publication meets the minimum
requirements of American National Standard for Information Sciences—Permanence of Paper for Printed Library Materials, ANSI Z39.48-1992. ∞

Library of Congress Cataloging-in-Publication Data
Garlock, Kristen L.
   Designing Web interfaces to library services and
resources / by Kristen L. Garlock, Sherry Piontek.
      p.   cm.
   Includes bibliographical references and index.
   ISBN 0-8389-0742-3
   1. Web sites—Design.   2. Library information
networks.   3. Web sites—United States—Design.
4. Library information networks—United States.
I. Piontek, Sherry.   II. Title.
Z674.75.W67G38   1999
005.7'2—dc21   98-37981

Printed in the United States of America.

03   02   01   00   99   5   4   3   2   1

Contents

Preface

Library web sites have become critical access points to library resources for many patrons. It is no longer enough to provide simple links to web resources. The proliferation of web-based Internet resources and the increasing technical sophistication of library patrons demand that librarians provide accessible and attractive interfaces to these resources.

Designing Web Interfaces to Library Services and Resources is intended for designers of web interfaces who have mastered HTML skills and are ready to tackle larger issues of interface design. This includes librarians who are interested not only in making their library web site interface more attractive and helpful to their patrons but who are also interested in learning more about the possibilities of moving beyond a basic web site to one that is more complex.

This book offers creative solutions for making the design of your site interesting for your users. We discuss issues surrounding the presentation of content and establishment of web-based services, highlighting the importance of web accessibility for all patrons. We also show you how to most effectively integrate user feedback so that your library's site truly serves its target audience. Practical tips for designing and supporting web interfaces and examples of innovative web-based resources are included in each chapter.

We are currently working with JSTOR, a not-for-profit organization involved in a cooperative venture with libraries and publishers. Our mission is to work with the publishers to digitize the backfiles of scholarly journals and provide this material to participating academic institutions via the World Wide Web. As JSTOR User Services Coordinators, we work extensively with contacts from participating sites, and the work we do on our web pages closely reflects the feedback we receive from our users. We have learned from experience which features librarians, scholars, and students have found useful, and which features required further development. We also work closely with technical staff in the design and implementation of new system features. In doing so, we have learned much about the evaluation of emerging technologies.

So much has been accomplished in such a short period of time. We have been encouraged by the evolution of library web sites over the past two years. It is exciting to see librarians taking a leadership role in creating sophisticated and useful web resources. Many librarian-designed sites are showcased in this book. By exploring these examples and the accompanying suggestions we hope that you will be inspired by the work of your colleagues.

1 Web Interface Design for Libraries

It has become clear to most World Wide Web users that the Web is in desperate need of informational sites that have been designed with the user in mind. In spite of an abundance of beautifully arranged pages, users still have a hard time finding sites that are efficient: efficient in the time it takes to navigate them, in their completeness of information, and in terms of their accessibility. In the library world especially, there is a widespread need for cleanly designed, functional web pages that are efficient and useful to the visitor looking for information.

In this book we will be moving beyond basic web page design to a discussion of guidelines for creating interfaces that maximize user satisfaction with web sites. We have seen a proliferation of library web pages in the past two years and have found that many libraries have at least a basic informational page available. In many cases, libraries are beginning to create complex sites incorporating more advanced designs and technologies. We have surveyed library pages for principles of good web design, have looked at other work that is emerging on sites throughout the Web, and gleaned principles from usability studies. We have also learned much about web design from our own experience with JSTOR, a web-based archive of scholarly journals that now has more than 300 participating libraries.

What Is Web Design?

As use of the Web has become increasingly important to libraries, librarians have started to find themselves in the business of "web design," often without having a clear grasp of what web design actually is. What does web design mean for librarians? A large part of designing a library web site is the organization of information, which is the traditional strength of librarians. In addition to information organization, there are other facets of web design that are equally important for librarians taking on the task of creating sites:

- **Technology.** Some knowledge of the appropriate technology needs to be part of a web designer's repertoire. In addition to knowing HTML, librarians who find themselves serving as web designers will need to know something about web protocols, browsers, the technical aspects of graphics, and alternative options available for presenting information in various formats. They will also need to stay abreast of new developments in these areas.

- **Graphic design.** As librarians have started creating more elaborate displays of information, they have naturally started to get involved in making their web pages look good. Designing web sites has led some librarians to look to the areas of graphic design and page layout for ideas and tips on making their web pages more attractive. Librarians are also starting to put together web pages with design tips for each other as they learn about what works and what doesn't work for them. For example, Macquarie University Library shares web design tips at **http://www.library.mq.edu.au/Using/ guidelines.html**.

- **Dynamism.** Web sites are never finished and will need to be updated frequently, in their content and in their design. Web sites are expected to be timely. This makes web design an activity that demands an intense degree of involvement, as well as a certain degree of flexibility, to be done well.

- **Creativity.** Web design is fundamentally a challenge: how to make information available in an original way for a large volume of users while employing the limited capabilities of HTML tagging. Typically, this challenge includes trying to present coherent, readable text in a limited space with a degree of attractiveness that will make people want to read it.

Fortunately, there are many helpful resources available on each of these topics, in print and online, to make the task easier. It is important to keep in mind that, as with all the other information sources in your library, the overall goal is to make the content accessible. This can be accomplished most effectively on your web site by keeping in mind these various elements of web design as you create and update your library's site.

What Do Web Users Want?

Years ago, as the use of personal computers was becoming more prevalent, the problem of user satisfaction was apparent in the development of computer software. There was a need for applications that an average user of a personal computer could understand and use comfortably, that is, "user-friendly" software. To that end, the field of usability engineering emerged, and it is now a professional discipline in which researchers develop and implement techniques for making software systems easier for end users. In this field, professionals employ standardized methods for studying users—such as controlled experiments, passive observation, and user surveys—with the intention of learning how users behave with software, and thereby improving their programs.

The phenomenal growth of the World Wide Web has resulted in the creation of millions of web sites, only some of which can truly be considered user-friendly. It seems only natural to wonder if principles from the field of usability engineering can be applied to web design. Our experience

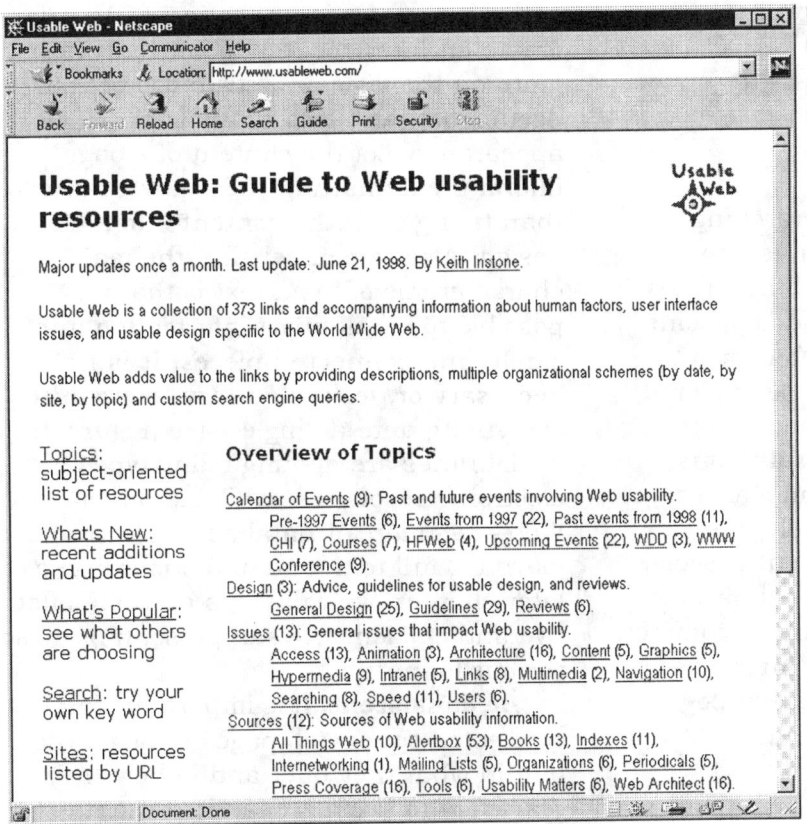

FIGURE 1.1
Usable Web provides links to many web design resources; http://www.usableweb.com/

is that while much of the information that has been gathered in software usability studies is irrelevant to the creation of web sites, some of it can be exceedingly helpful to those who are trying to carefully plan a web interface for their site. Furthermore, as the field of web design expands, a unique body of knowledge is accumulating about the principles that lead to usable web sites (see the Appendix).

One site that argues for the application of usability engineering principles to web site design is Usable Web: Guide to Web Usability Resources (**http://www. usableweb.com**), which is "a collection of 228 links and accompanying information about human factors, user interface issues, and usable design specific to the World Wide Web." This site focuses on the need for understanding web site users, promoting usable designs, solving usability problems, and understanding other constraints in web development (Figure 1.1). It is easy to see that all of these factors are just as important to web design as they are to the design of software.

On the other hand, there is some evidence to suggest that not all software usability principles can be applied to web design. *Web Site Usability: A Designer's Guide* (**http://world.std.com/~uieweb/ bookdesc.htm**), for example, is a recent report based on usability tests conducted by User Interface Engineering, a research and consulting firm in North Andover, Massachusetts. User Interface Engineering observed more than 50 people as they searched for information on nine popular web sites. They discovered that the sites users said they liked best were not necessarily the sites they used the most effectively, in contrast to application software where results suggest that users like best the software they use the most easily. It may be more important then to create a web site that is attractive and up-to-date in its content than one that strictly follows traditional interface design guidelines.

Creating a Good User Interface in the Web Environment

We have developed some overarching principles that can guide you as you create more sophisticated web interfaces, some drawn from usability studies, some from the emerging field of web design. Many of these principles will be explored in more detail in later chapters.

Plan your structure carefully. It is natural to want to jump in and start creating a web interface immediately, but following a carefully thought out process will provide a much more logical basis for your web site interface. There is a common paradigm used in the field of interface design that may also be helpful in beginning the design of a web interface:

- Statement of the problem (What information will the web site contain?)

- Target audience (Who will this web site target?)

- Information organization (How will this web site be organized?)

- User interface (What will this site look like?)

In this model, each step is necessary for creating a strong foundation upon which to build your site. Building an interface upon solid decisions leads to a more successful design whether it is an interface for software or a web site.

Let content inform design. An interface should allow the user to focus on the task of discovering the content within a site, and should not have features that distract from the main goal of finding information. This, obviously, is very important for a library's site where information gathering is of primary concern. As you create an interface, try to concentrate more on the logic and structure of your documents, and less on their physical appearance. Let the content of a page inform the formatting of the page, rather than trying to fit the content into a flashy design. Also remember that the main characteristic of hypertext is that it is possible to break apart information into small, interconnected pieces. It is not necessary or desirable to try to organize everything onto a single page (Figure 1.2).

Libraries are making many types of electronic resources available on the Web—commercial databases, electronic journals, full text, and much more. In a later chapter, we will focus on some effective and efficient ways of presenting these various formats.

Be consistent. It is important for a connected set of web pages to be consistent in what they offer and in how they react. Try to avoid a chaotic presentation by striving for a visually unified, consistent "look and feel" in your web site. Readers who are eager to get to the information on a site may eventually learn to navigate through it no matter how bad the design is, but it is obviously an advantage to make navigation simple. If users do not learn to navigate through the site, they will not return to it. Consistency is a key element to learnability in any situation, so using predictable navigational conventions and a consistent look will make it easier for your users to develop reliable expectations about your site and the information it contains.

We will be going into more detail about some of the elements that contribute to consistency in web interface design in later chapters. These elements will include:

- Using color and page layout to integrate your pages

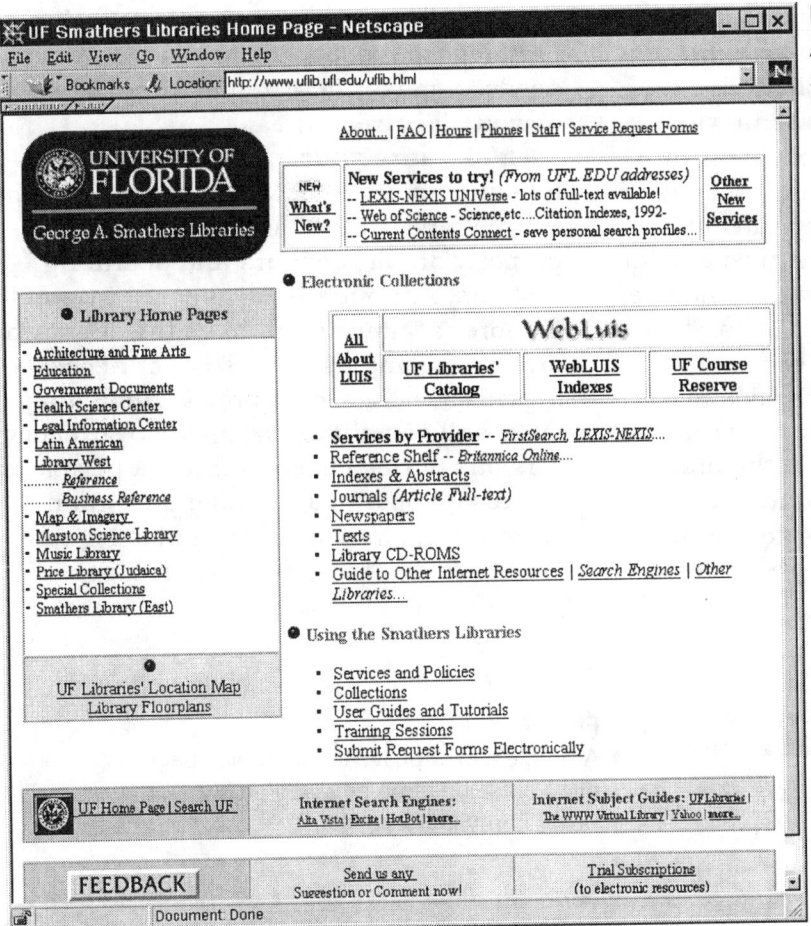

FIGURE 1.2
A main page with links to subsequent pages; http://www.uflib.ufl.edu/uflib.html

- Using color in ways that will guarantee consistent display on all browsers and operating systems

- Using design elements tailored for your target audience

Create an intuitive web site. In addition to being consistent, one of the most critical aspects of user interface design lies in the use of familiar models. As you design your web interface, familiarize yourself with the Web in general. Design your site to minimize the mistakes a user can make by visiting other web sites and noting what mistakes you made as you tried to use them. When in doubt about how to present certain types of information on your site, follow convention—don't make your page so different from all other pages that people feel they need to learn new skills just to access the information you promise. More and more frequently, users tend to see the Web as a single resource—they are searching "The Web," not just your site. This often means that the feature you think is a great interface innovation may be seen by your users as an impediment to the information they need.

Another important aspect of creating an intuitive web site is to organize logically. One way of doing this is to present simple information first and then progress into more complex information. A web site with multiple layers of information should offer a few simple, categorical sections and then branch into specifics. It is better to present your reader with a predictable, well-organized hierarchy of pages than with pages connected randomly (Figure 1.3).

Similarly, it is important to let the user know what actions are appropriate on any given page. Try to imagine the user's point of view at various locations within the site, and try to anticipate any possible ambiguity. For example, a search page needs to make it clear where the user needs to enter information, and in what form the information needs to appear. If the first page of a multiple-page document is displayed, it needs to be clear to the user how to move to the second page. A page that requires an external action, such as bringing up a sound file or an image, needs to make these required actions obvious (Figure 1.4).

Make sure your interface is compatible and accessible. It is always important to create pages that are going to display properly on all browsers and operating systems. Although Netscape and Internet Explorer at times seem to be the only web browsers being used, this is not necessarily the case. Text-only browsers such as Lynx still remain amazingly active. Older versions of Netscape and Internet Explorer will also display pages differently than more recent versions. It can also be surprising to see the difference in display

FIGURE 1.3
A simple and effective top-level web page; http://battalion.tamu.edu/web/archives/BushLibrary/index.html

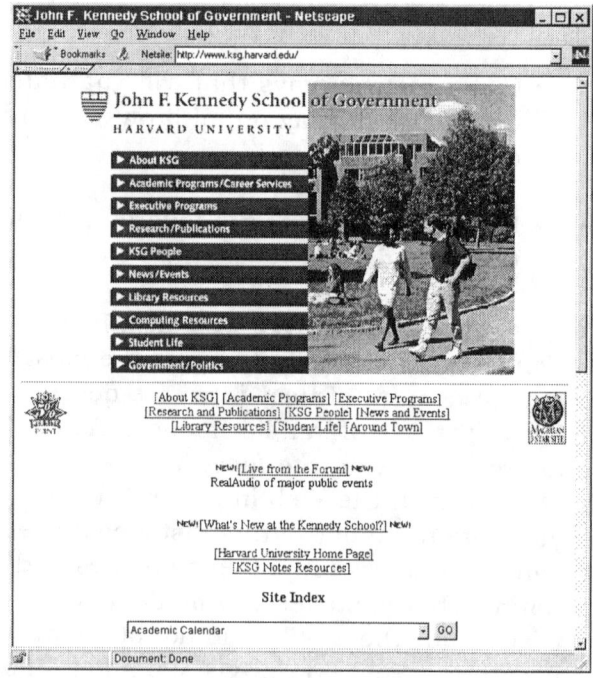

FIGURE 1.4
Real Audio files may be added to a web page; http://www.ksg.harvard.edu

between a Macintosh, a PC, or a UNIX workstation. The point is, even though your page looks the way you want it to look on your own machine and your particular web browser, be aware of the variations that can affect the way your users see it. Try to view your web pages on as many platforms as possible to get an idea of the variations your users might see.

It is also very important to be aware of connection speed differences as you create your web site. Slow speed may be the single biggest impediment to user satisfaction on the Web. Remember that many of your patrons will be accessing your pages from home or travel via modem. Slow-loading pages are frustrating, and many users will just stop or cancel a page to go to a different site rather than wait. Even though modems are becoming faster, they still lag behind the direct connections of most libraries. This awareness of speed constraints should affect such decisions as the number of images you place on your pages and the size of these images, as well as the amount of text you place on a single page. You may also want to consider creating alternative, low-bandwidth versions of your pages.

There are many other issues that affect accessibility on the Web. In Chapter 5 we will discuss:

- The need to be aware of users with physical impairments and the special equipment they may use to read web pages

- Specific issues that affect access for all users: graphics, tagging, and document structure

- How to include graphics, video, and audio in accessible ways

- How to determine your site's overall accessibility

Provide a solid navigational base. Web sites allow readers to choose and create their own course of information gathering. Thus, it is very important that you provide them with signs and markers along the way. Users should, at the very least, be able to find their way back to the first page of your site. Ideally, they should be able to formulate a rough map of your site in their minds as they move from page to page.

Later on, we will be detailing some of the most important elements of navigation:

- How to provide multiple levels of navigational support to accommodate the first-time user as well as the experienced searcher

- Where to include the navigational elements users have come to expect on web pages

- How to ensure that all of your library's web pages provide consistent navigation

Design your interface for your audience. It is your responsibility to make good choices about the appropriateness of the interface to match the user and material. You want to operate at the level of your audience. Don't patronize or be afraid of complexity. Users can understand complexity when it is necessary to get to levels of complex information—it is frivolous complexity of design that is frustrating. It is also important to remember that more and more of your users are experienced in web navigation, so basic directions ("Click on this link") are unnecessary.

Put user input into perspective. Continuous user input ensures that you have a good understanding of what users want to find and what they want to do when they reach your site, and how well your design satisfies their needs. As you receive feedback about your web site, though, do not implement suggestions indiscriminately—some of them just might not be any good! Take suggestions into account, but try to be reasonable about the changes you make, and have good reasons for making them.

We will be discussing other aspects of user input in a later chapter:

- How to effectively incorporate user response into the iterative design process

- How to gather useful feedback from your users

- How to understand and make the most of web usage statistics

Be aware of the dynamic nature of the Web. All web pages date quickly—don't expect yours ever to be finished. The main lesson that anyone learns while working on a web site is that there will always be a need for changes and updates in the information it contains. Furthermore, the Web itself is always changing. New technologies are being developed, new browser capabilities are implemented, and HTML is evolving. All of these things will affect the timeliness of your web interface.

In a later chapter, we will discuss ways of moving forward with your web pages by:

- Providing newer, "high-tech" services

- Considering alternatives and supplements to HTML: JavaScript, PDF, RealAudio, and Shockwave

- Creatively using new technologies to aid in resource presentation

As you design your web interface, always focus first on content, presentation, navigation, and compatibility, rather than on typography or layout. Be on the lookout for new and creative ways to employ web technologies in areas such as document navigation and stylistic consistency. And always design with the needs of your audience foremost in mind.

2 Content

Content is the most important element of a web site. Useful information is what distinguishes a great web site from the insignificant ones. Most initial versions of library web sites include typical information such as hours, policies, and links to Internet resources. However, these minimal pages do not provide access to many library resources and services. Patrons still need to go to the library building in order to access most resources, including the library catalog, CD-ROM databases, reference tools, and local materials. Many libraries are now ready to move to the next stage of web development: providing resources and services to their patrons via the library's online presence. Technologies are now readily available which allow libraries to make local resources available through web interfaces, and many commercial resource providers offer web interfaces to their products. With the popularity of home computing and the widespread availability of affordable Internet access, patrons now have the technical capability and skills to access many of their library's resources from home, if those resources are available online.

Ideas for a Content-Rich Site

Online Catalogs

For several years, libraries wanting to make their online catalogs available to Internet users have made them available via telnet or tn3270 connections. Accessing library catalogs through these types of connections requires telnet or tn3270 software. These days, many patrons accessing library resources both at home and in the library will be doing so through the library web page using a graphical web browser. In order to access the library's catalog through a telnet connection, patrons still need to acquire and install telnet/tn3270 software in addition to their browser software.

With the advent of web interfaces to library catalogs, an additional access method is now available. Web-based library catalog interfaces offer several advantages over telnet access, but many are still in the earliest stages of development. For this reason, many libraries have recently added a web interface option to their online catalog but continue to offer some type of telnet connection as well. A great advantage to web interfaces to library catalogs is that they allow users to access the catalog without installing extra software. Another benefit to a web-based catalog is the ability to include hyperlinks to online resources which permit patrons to jump directly to Internet resources listed in the library catalog (Figure 2.1). Other appealing features of a web-based catalog include bookmarking of items, easy-to-use interfaces, hyperlinked subject headings, and more flexibility for including and formatting help files and online feedback options.

Web interfaces to library catalogs do have their drawbacks. Partly because of limitations inherent in the design of the Web, many interfaces currently have limited functionality, and modifying the interface for your local needs can be difficult. The ability to store searches, connect to indexes or other databases, and include detailed library holdings may not be available, depending on the product. However, while web gateways to online catalogs may not include all the functionality of the previous systems, they are evolving quickly as the popularity of the Web increases.

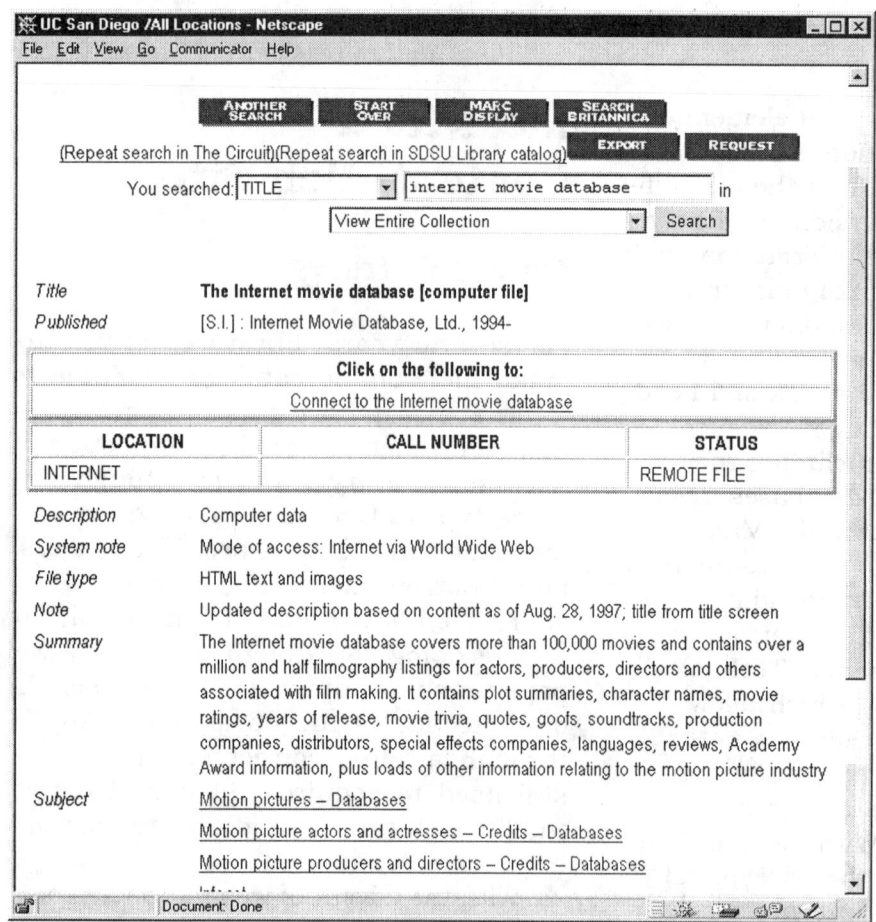

FIGURE 2.1
An online catalog with links to Internet resources;
http://roger.ucsd.edu/

Commercial Indexes and Databases

Commercial indexes and databases, which have long been available in formats such as print, floppy disks, or CD-ROMs, are now accessible through the Web. Like web-based online catalogs, web-accessible commercial databases have their advantages and disadvantages. Web-based databases can make it possible for patrons to access resources from outside the library building, and Internet-savvy patrons feel comfortable with a web browser as a medium for using the databases. Unlike materials in other formats, web-based collections offer more flexibility for access.

However, dealing with web-based products does present some challenges. Linking to items within databases, such as individual journals within electronic journal collections, may be desirable but difficult to accomplish. Ownership of the materials is also an important issue. Some commercial resource providers grant ownership of the materials to the libraries, guaranteeing perpetual access to the material or supplying the library with a copy of the material in a different format. However, not all vendors guarantee ownership of the materials to libraries. Also, products available in various formats may require increased fees for the electronic versions.

Internet Resources

The Internet has often been described as chaotic and criticized for the lack of reliable and accurate resources. While the number of badly designed and insubstantial sites may not diminish, the amount of resources of value and access to them have dramatically increased. Useful Internet sites are now created, organized, and evaluated by librarians and other committed web developers (Figure 2.2). Web site creators and managers now have many sources they may rely upon for information about web resources of interest to their users. Search tools and web directories, both specialized and general, permit better searches for Internet resources. Many print and online magazines offer thoughtful reviews of web sites. Well-established companies, educational institutions, and individuals now produce web-based resources—everyone from L.L. Bean to the White House has joined the Web community.

Local Resources

In the early days of the Web, transferring local resources, such as library newsletters and instructional handouts, to the

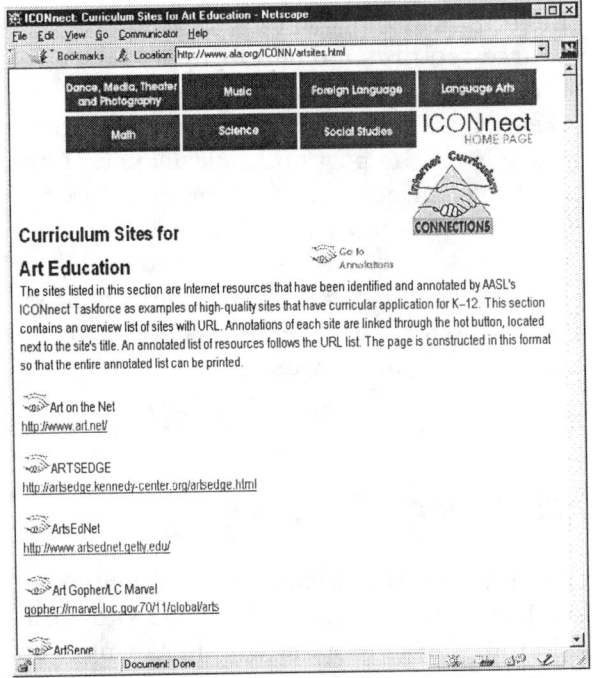

FIGURE 2.2

A directory of art sites evaluated by specialists for a specific audience; http://www.ala.org/ICONN/artsites.html

Internet often meant a potentially painful conversion process that sacrificed much of the original document formatting. Web-builder tools developed over the past couple of years now make it easier than ever to make local resources available through the Web. These tools also enable web page creators to retain or improve the format and enhance accessibility to the materials. Print resources, community information files, image collections, and other library-specific resources may all be considered potential web resources. Conversion is easier than ever due to commercial vendors who provide ready-to-use servers and other Internet software, web gateways to database software, and special tools and software such as HTML editors that include toolbar options for designing advanced HTML features.

Presenting Content

Each individual type of web-based resource requires a different approach to presentation. Some resources will be created in-house and will involve creative choices on the part of the developers. Other content will consist of commercial products purchased by the library. There are some universal issues surrounding all web resources which should be considered when creating or selecting content to include on your pages.

Technical Support

As you plan the presentation of commercial and local materials on your site, you should also determine whether or not you will need some kind of technical support for installing or maintaining your resource. Commercial resources which

feature built-in web interfaces generally do not necessitate extensive technical support on the part of the library. Setting up access to the resources may require only adding a link to the resource from a web page or pages. However, if the resource requires the use of a special helper application, it may be necessary to enlist the help of a technical support person to load the extra software on multiple workstations or on a server.

If you plan to include links to resources such bibliographic indexes in the interface to your web-based library catalog, you may need technical assistance to install and maintain the resources. The material, often in the format of a tape or CD-ROM, will need to be loaded on a server. Often, interfaces to this material need to be modified or adapted to fit your needs and the specifications of your system. Technical support will be a continuing need. As the resources are updated, the new data will need to be loaded onto the system, and modifications of system hardware and software may require changes to the resource interface and structure.

You may also require technical support if you plan to implement a complex or extensive local resource, such as a web-accessible local database. Technology professionals will be in the best position to select the appropriate software, ensure the compatibility of the software with your network, manipulate the software, and convert the materials to the appropriate format. If you have the technical background, or if you have in-house programmers and technical support staff, you are in good position to create and implement some great resources for your library web site.

A helpful approach to creating or setting up a new resource is to form a development team early in the design or implementation process. Here are some tips for getting started:

- Consider identifying a librarian and a technical support staff member as the "point" people for a project

- Implement a team approach that remains consistent throughout development of the resource

- Make sure that the purpose of the resource is understood by every team member

- Involve librarians throughout the process as designers, technical staff, or organizers

Format

Just as in a traditional library collection, a library web site will include materials in different formats. ASCII text, HTML documents, images, movies, and databases are all typical formats for Internet resources. When creating your own web-based content, you should consider your options and select the format most appropriate to the content. With commercial resources you will have less control over format, but you should be sure that you can understand and manage the format of the resources you select.

Choosing Format

When creating your own resources, it is almost always necessary to migrate local content from an existing format to another. An obvious example is printed material. Print documents may be scanned and converted to an HTML document, or if they exist in a digital format, it may only be necessary to tag the material. However, converting a document to HTML format may be impractical in some cases if the document is very long or is of secondary importance. A better format in this case may be a PDF file. Both text documents and images may be converted to PDF format. Accessing PDF documents does require the use of a helper application such as Adobe Acrobat Reader, software that is available for multiple platforms and is already a widely used application. A library manual, annual report, or archive of meeting minutes could require a major investment of tagging time for items that may be used only sporadically. PDF conversion of these types of documents is simple and more time efficient. The documents are easily accessible and if they are converted text, may even be searchable. The PDF format is also very useful for those documents whose formatting is important to keep intact. Forms, handouts, and maps may be presented exactly as they appear in print (Figure 2.3).

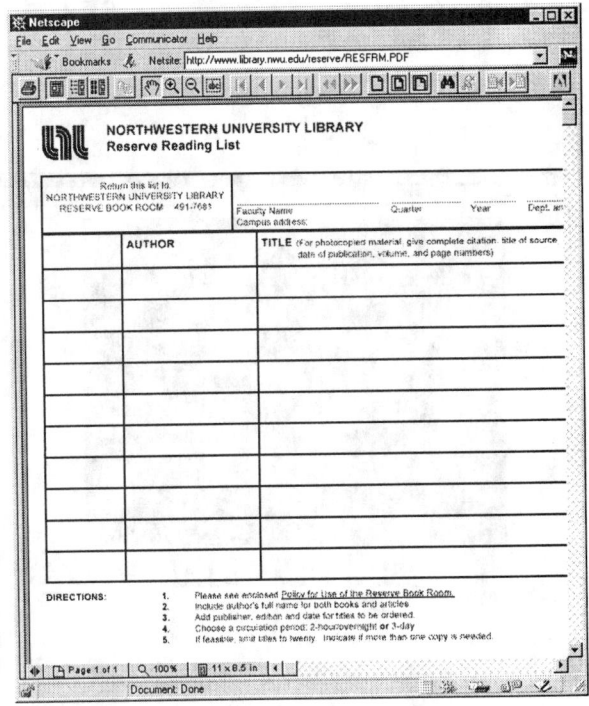

FIGURE 2.3
As a PDF document, this form is available via the web with its original formatting intact; http://www.library.nwu.edu/reserve/RESFRM.PDF

Documents such as, word processing files, spreadsheets, and slide presentations can be easily included on your site. Many conversion tools are now available which are designed to work with the software applications used to produce these documents. Some conversion tools are provided by the software manufacturer and others are created by independent software designers. You may download applications from the Microsoft web site which do a very good job at converting EXCEL spreadsheets, Word documents, and PowerPoint presentations to web formats (Figure 2.4). Once downloaded, the applications become options in the main software toolbars. Rather than maintaining separate HTML documents for these items, which must be updated in addition to the original document, it is now possible to maintain the original document and easily convert it each time it is updated. If necessary, you may also edit the HTML versions after they have been converted using any HTML or text editor.

Many databases produced with popular software packages may now be accessed via the Web. FileMaker Pro 4.0 offers a built-in feature that allows FileMaker databases to be accessed and modified through a web interface (Figure 2.5). Separate products also exist which act as gateways between FileMaker Pro and the Web.

Presenting materials in multiple formats will increase the usability of your site. Help files are an excellent example. In addition to HTML versions of help files for online use, you may choose to offer a PDF format which may be printed for later use for those who prefer to work from printed materials. Presenting materials in multiple formats is also a good idea for accessibility reasons. PDF documents are a great choice for certain types of items, but PDF currently is not very accessible to people using screen readers. Essential documents and other important information should be available in a format which is accessible to your entire audience.

Access

Structure

Access to information will be influenced by the format and purpose of the material. Access is a critical area that should be given careful consideration and plenty of planning time. If your patrons cannot easily locate and use the content on your site, it is as if the content does not exist. Three main issues are integral components of access regardless of the type of material: structure, awareness, and restrictions.

The structure of access refers to how access to a resource is organized—the access method. The access structures for each resource should be designed while keeping the research behavior of the

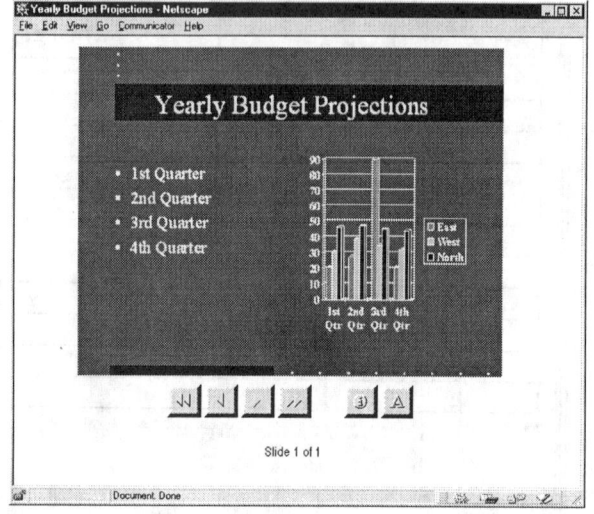

FIGURE 2.4
Sample PowerPoint presentation saved as an HTML document

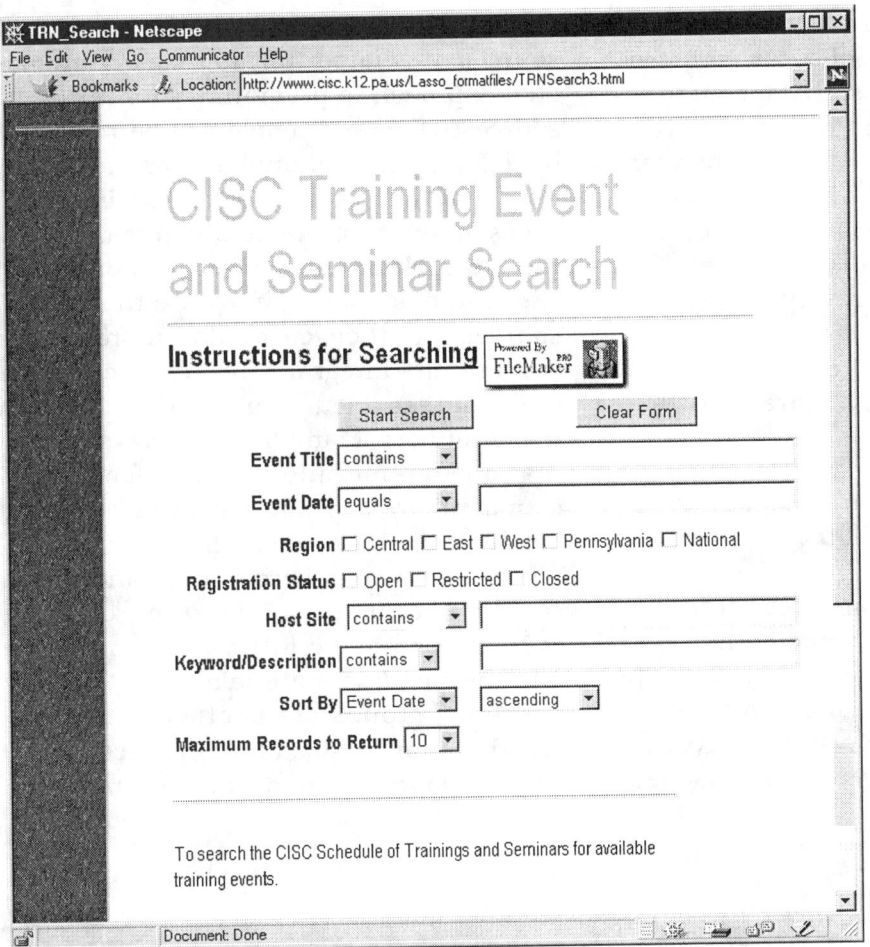

FIGURE 2.5

A FileMaker Pro database accessible via a web interface;
http://www.cisc.k12.pa.us/Lasso_formatfiles/TRNSearch3.html

audience in mind. Electronic journal collections may serve as an illustration of this point. Libraries subscribing to a collection or multiple collections of electronic journals often list these collections on their web site, sometimes with a short summary listing the focus and coverage of the journal collections. A short description is essential, as most patrons will not be aware of the difference in holdings and coverage of each different collection. Users may not know in which collection their journal is located. They only want to access the specific article needed for their research in the easiest way possible.

A better access structure for a journal collection is a journal-level directory, rather than collection-level approach. A hyperlinked directory of titles presents both the designer and users with several options. The directory may be organized alphabetically (best for people looking for a particular article) or by discipline according to a library scheme (best for those interested in browsing titles in a subject area). A combination of these methods is the most accessible scheme. Hyperlinks allow journals to be listed in multiple subject or departmental areas and to be accessed by people with different needs.

A search mechanism could also be considered another type of access structure. Search mechanisms are, of course, most often utilized when the format of the material is a database. Search mechanisms may also serve as access tools for locating other formats of resources in addition to databases. If you subscribe to journal collections that include a very large number of journals, you may want to allow searching of your journal directories as an additional access option (Figure 2.6).

Getting the Word Out

Another essential component of access is awareness. As you add or modify the features of your site, it will be necessary to promote the resources to make your users aware of their availability. Different types of libraries may require different approaches

for getting the word out about new resources. It is important to take a multifaceted approach to promoting your resources. Different people will be reached by different promotional approaches.

If you maintain an academic library web site, the best way to promote the use of the research-oriented resources on your site is to help faculty integrate the resources into their curricula. In order to successfully integrate the resources into their courses, faculty must be familiar with the resources. Many libraries have found that one-on-one tutorials with faculty members are very successful in helping faculty learn how to use the resources. When faculty members understand the scope and structure of the resource, they will then be able to integrate the resource into their course materials.

E-mail groups are another excellent tool that may be used to announce web site developments and new resources.

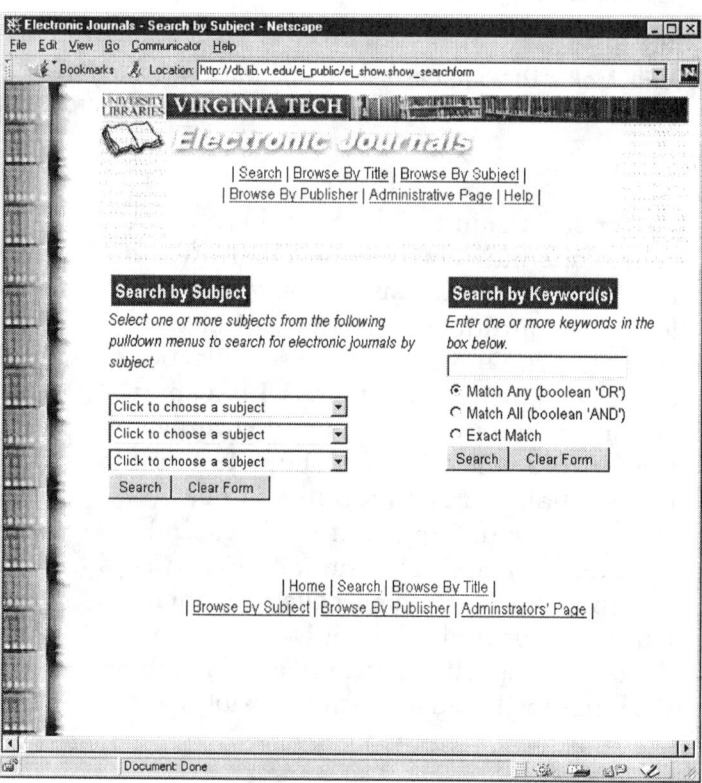

FIGURE 2.6
A collection of electronic journals accessible via a subject or keyword search; http://db.lib.vt.edu/ej_public/ej_show. show_searchform

Sending announcements to existing e-mail groups for courses, department e-mail lists, and student lists can be very effective. You may also want to consider creating a general e-mail group for people interested in library news and developments. Launching an e-mail list can be as simple as allowing people to sign up using a traditional sign-up sheet and creating a group using available software options. Many e-mail software packages will allow you to create e-mail groups for large mailings. A more sophisticated approach would be implementing an announcement listserv, which may require a larger investment of time and money, but would offer greater flexibility as patrons could add and remove themselves as they wish.

It is important to publicize the availability of your web resources and services via traditional means. Library newsletters, posters, flyers, bookmarks, student newspapers, and bibliographic instruction sessions can all be used effectively to promote online library resources. These tools can be especially useful in attracting first-time users to your web site. E-mail groups and announcements on web pages will not be seen by patrons who have not yet visited your library web site or are just beginning to learn how to use web resources.

Finally, good web site organization is key to facilitating content awareness. If your resources are organized in a logical manner that is appropriate to the content, then people will be able to locate them. Links to important and heavily used resources should be placed on the main page and at the tops of pages. You may also want to consider adding a "What's New" section to your site (Figure 2.7). A "What's New" page can include announcements and highlights of new resources with links and descriptions. If this section is always up-to-date, your users will come to rely on it to learn about site developments and new resources.

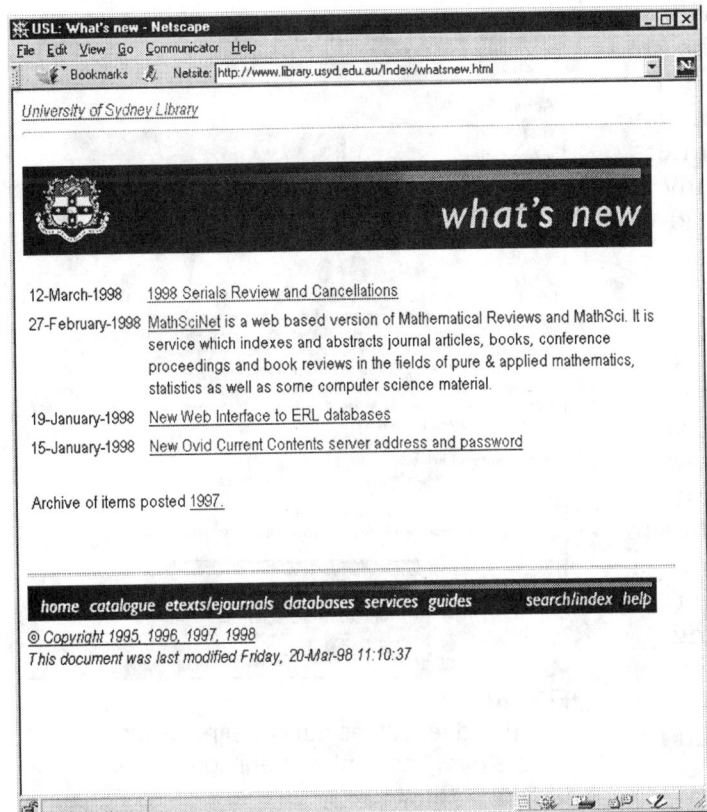

FIGURE 2.7
A "What's New" page lists important web site developments; http://www.library.usyd.edu.au/Index/whatsnew.html

Restrictions

Restrictions are another issue related to content. Certain resources will be available only to limited audiences. Vendor-imposed restrictions are required for most commercial resources. In public libraries, these resources will generally be restricted to library cardholders and patrons using the resource at the library. In academic libraries, a site license agreement may allow use by patrons located at the library, across campus, and at home. Sometimes, however, more specific restrictions will apply. The resource may be limited to use at the library only, limited to use at one workstation, or may be used by staff only on the behalf of the patron. For other resources, restrictions may be applied by the library itself because the technical capability or staff to support access beyond the physical library is not available.

Restrictions may be handled in several ways. Web resources are usually restricted to use at a particular site, by limiting use to those who access the resource from within a specific IP (Internet Protocol) range. Each machine connected to the Internet has a specific IP address. The IP addresses may be static, in which case one fixed IP address is assigned to each Internet-accessible workstation, or they may be dynamic in which case a group of IP addresses is assigned to a group of computers; the computers are assigned an IP address from within the range as they connect to the Internet. This IP information is entered into the access file on the vendor's server, which then allows access only from the valid range of IP addresses. This type of access is easy to set up but does have limitations. If a library wishes to allow access by patrons from nonlibrary or off-campus locations, it must have some mechanism in place for authenticating legitimate users. This may be a dial-in system that allows users to dial in to a server which then assigns them a valid IP address, or it may be some sort of a username/password system.

If restrictions do apply to the resource, it is important to post these restrictions in an obvious area on your site (Figure 2.8). If special access instructions are needed to use the resource from a remote location, this information will be especially important. As more and more library users obtain nonlibrary and nonuniversity accounts through local Internet service providers and commercial services such as America Online, they will want to use these resources from home.

Delivery

Delivery of web resources is defined by the format of the materials, which may also impose delivery restrictions. Common options for delivery of materials include online viewing, printing, downloading, and sending of materials through e-mail.

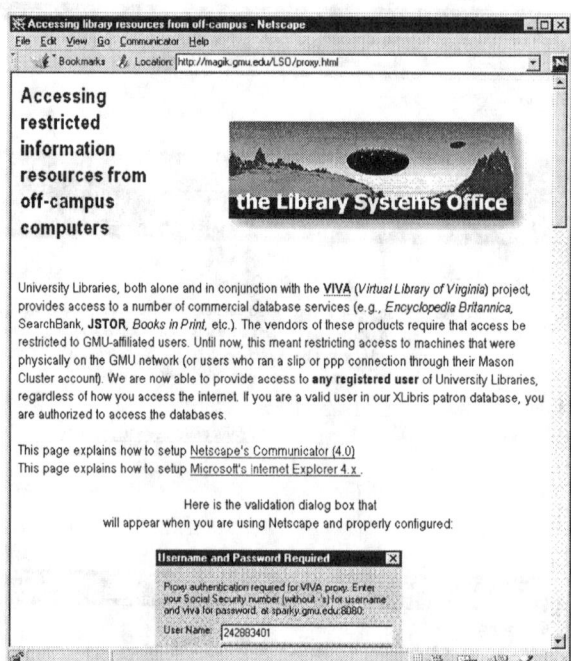

FIGURE 2.8
Restricted resources may require special access directions; http://magik.gmu.edu/LSO/proxy.html

Online Viewing

Nearly every resource will offer an online viewing option. ASCII text, HTML files, PDF files, images, and many other types of documents may be viewed within web browsers. However, some files, such as audio files and video clips, do require the use of special helper applications. If you include resources on your site that require the use of a helper application, include links to downloading the software and directions for accessing the material.

Printing

Web documents may often be printed using the browser print command, but this does not always produce optimal results. Sometimes it may be necessary to provide a special printing tool along with your resource. For example, printing PDF files requires the use of Acrobat Reader. Again, you should always include a link to any external applications needed for using the resource.

Downloading

Downloading is a popular feature with library users. Many people do initial research at libraries but prefer to continue work at home or in a computer lab. If they can download the information to a floppy disk, they will be able to take it with them to a remote location and use it at a later date. Certain downloading options may be available using browser features. ASCII text, HTML documents, and individual images can be easily downloaded using built-in browser options. Other materials such as software or large files can be compressed for easier downloading and portability.

Policy restrictions for commercial resources may preclude the downloading of certain materials. Format may also impose restrictions on downloading files. It may be possible to download large files from a library web site directly to a hard drive. However, patrons using the resource at the library will not be able to save large files to a floppy disk for later use. If you do permit downloading of files, include file size information with the material to be downloaded.

E-mail

In addition to printing and downloading materials, another delivery option is sending material through e-mail. Some commercial resources, such as IAC's SearchBank, allow registered users to request abstracts and full-text information to be sent to an e-mail address. Alternatively, if you are running a server with local information, you may be able to set up an e-mailing option for your materials. Browser "mail document" options may also be used to deliver text files via e-mail. Online help files may be needed to bring this option to the attention of your users.

Helper Applications

Some types of materials may require additional software for delivery to the user. Certain image formats, movie formats, printing formats, and audio files cannot be handled with browsers and can only be accessed via additional software. This additional software is often called a "helper application." A common example of a helper application is Adobe Acrobat Reader, required for accessing PDF files. Another example is RealPlayer, which is required for accessing RealAudio and RealVideo files.

If you decide to include materials on your site which require the use of a helper application, it is a good idea to include a link to a site where users may acquire the software. Help files or downloading instructions should also be included.

User Assistance

User assistance is an important part of a well-designed web site. It may be presented in the form of contact information for support services (via e-mail, phone, or fax) or in the form of online help files, immediately accessible information about using the resource. The best approach is to provide a combination of the two, online help information and contact information for further questions.

Contact information can be easily included. An address, telephone number, and/or e-mail address should be included in an obvious location. Encouraging questions to be submitted through an e-mail address may be the easiest way to handle them. This method allows the staff in charge of coordinating the replies more control over when and how the questions are answered. E-mail questions can also be submitted to one or more staff members, logged, and archived, which can be an important means of documenting user problems and developing standard replies.

A form for submission of questions can help both the user and the support person (Figure 2.9). Giving the user the opportunity to submit a free-form question or comment is important, and may be sufficient for most simple questions or brief comments. However, if a user is reporting

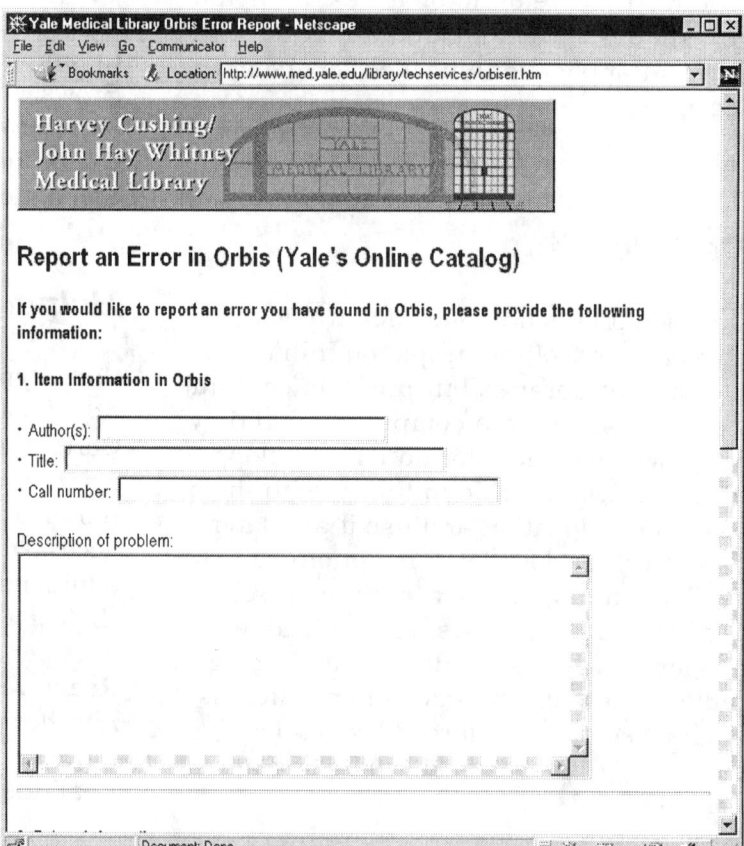

FIGURE 2.9
An online form for the submission of error reports; http://www.med.yale.edu/library/techservices/orbiserr.htm

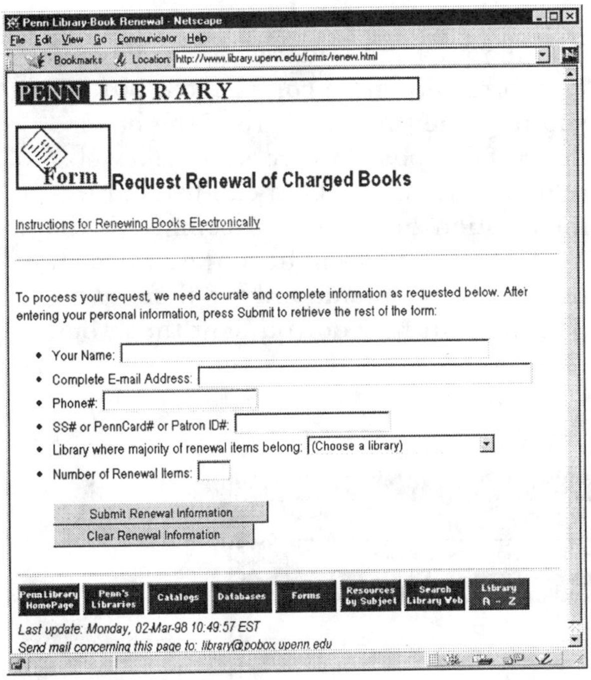

FIGURE 2.10
An online form for the renewal of library materials; http://www.library.upenn.edu/forms/renew.html

The layout and implementation of online help files should incorporate all the elements of good design. Simplicity, consistency, and convenience are keys to well-designed help files. The organization of the files should be easy to follow. If your resource is extensive or complex, you may want to offer context-sensitive help files throughout the system. Context-sensitive help files are those that are directly related to documents or features located at different points within the system. If you decide to include help files throughout the site, the format of the files should be consistent. Most important, the help files should be easy to locate.

Presenting Services

Circulation Services

Many libraries that provide a web interface to their online catalog also offer some level of circulation service as well. Placing materials on hold, reviewing items currently on loan, and renewing materials online are just some of the conveniences libraries offer their patrons (Figure 2.10). These features are integrated into online catalog systems and may be available via a web interface for patrons. The ability to access these services from home is received eagerly by patrons.

a problem or has a complicated question, a structured help form that requests specific details about the problem, the user's technical environment, and any error message received can be a useful tool. Offering guidance about the type of information required to diagnose a problem can reduce the need for an extended prediagnosis e-mail exchange, and allow the problem-solving process to be more efficient.

Web developers should offer some type of mechanism for the submission of user questions and should be prepared to respond to these questions. However, as a web developer you should also consider offering assistance in the form of online help files, which can be a proactive means of assisting patrons who are learning to use your resource and can help trouble-shoot problems that occur when using the resource. Unlike help provided over the telephone or through e-mail, online help files offer immediate assistance and allow your patrons to help themselves.

Digital Reference

Technically speaking, reference service is one of the easiest library services to offer electronically. No specialized equipment or software is required to accept and answer reference questions submitted through a web site. However, digital reference service can be one of the most challenging and time-consuming services to provide electronically because of the personnel and management issues associated with it. Before initiating a digital reference service, it is important to thoroughly consider what level of service will be provided, how the service will be provided, and who will respond to the questions.

The mechanism by which patrons submit reference questions may be as simple as an e-mail address, or may be a specially designed web form (Figure 2.11). Offering an e-mail address is easy, while web forms are more complicated but allow you to guide the structure of the questions. If composed appropriately, a web reference form can help capture more information in the initial communication.

Most libraries will have the time or the resources to respond only to their own patrons. But how do you limit the submis-

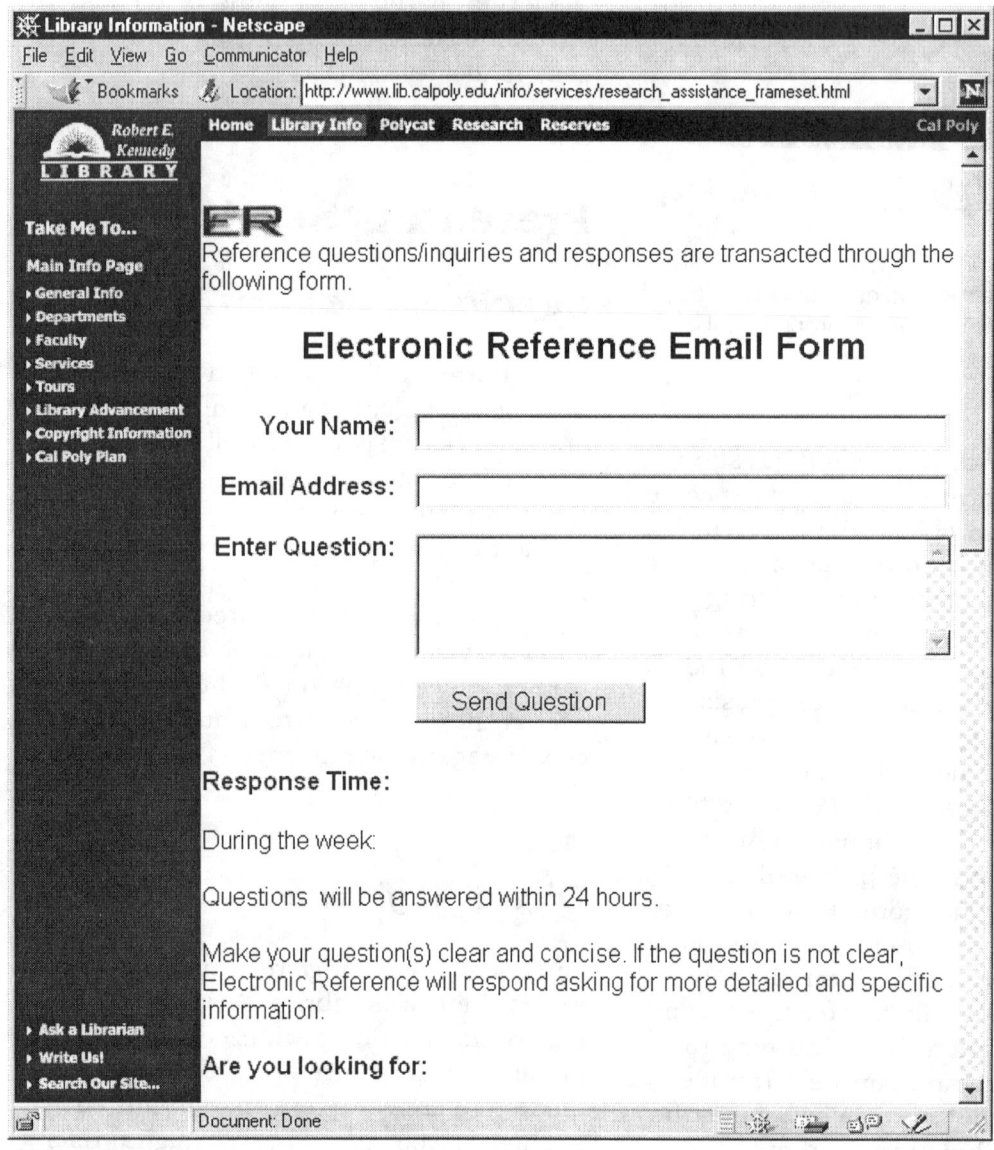

FIGURE 2.11
It is important to provide service details with an online reference form;
http://www.lib.calpoly.edu/info/services/research_assistance_frameset.html

sion of questions only to your library's patrons? Some libraries technically restrict the submission of the questions by requiring that patrons enter their library card number and a password in order to view the reference page. Other libraries choose to ask patrons to submit their library card or a similar ID number with the questions. This second approach has the potential drawback of placing the burden of verifying the questioner's affiliation on the library staff managing the questions.

In addition to deciding on a format and potential restrictions for the submission of the reference questions, it is necessary to decide how the questions will be managed once they are received. One approach is to appoint one person to be the coordinator of the electronic reference service. The coordinator does not necessarily respond to all questions submitted, but would be responsible for forwarding messages to the appropriate reference staff person, ensuring that the questions are answered in a timely manner and generally making sure that the service is running smoothly.

Perhaps the most difficult task involved with implementing a digital reference service is deciding what level of service will be offered. One option is to accept all reference questions submitted to the digital reference service. Another approach is to accept only "ready-reference" questions. This limitation on the nature of questions which may be asked can be difficult to enforce. Some libraries offer guidelines that illustrate the differences between ready-reference and in-depth questions, but these differences may be difficult for your patrons to distinguish.

Some libraries are experimenting with video reference services. Video reference does have advantages over an e-mail reference service. The interactions are closer to in-person interviews, the librarian is provided with visual clues in addition to the question, and the interview may

be carried out more efficiently in terms of time. However, video reference requires both the patron and the librarian to have access to the appropriate equipment. Most patrons do not have the technical capability to participate in a video reference interview. Video reference services are therefore best carried out in more controlled and technologically advanced environments, such as on campuses and in corporate libraries.

Electronic Course Reserves

Electronic course reserves, or e-reserves, is a growing area of online library services, especially as more instructors integrate Internet resources into their curriculum along with traditional course materials. The creation and maintenance of e-reserves collections can necessitate a large investment of time and resources on the part of the library and the faculty. Converting the materials, creating each course page, providing support for accessing the materials, and obtaining permission to use copyrighted materials are not insignificant tasks. However, the advantages of e-reserves services are numerous and many libraries are committing resources to their development.

One of the most attractive features of an e-reserves collection is the ability to integrate all types of curricular materials into one course resource. Internet resources, sample tests, lecture notes, assigned reading, presentations, and other material can be made available online. Multiple courses can use the same materials while reducing the need for duplication. Materials will not be lost or destroyed. And best of all, materials are accessible from a remote location and will never be unavailable because they are checked out by another patron.

Some libraries offering e-reserves services use homegrown systems to organize course materials, while other libraries use commercial products. Although a homegrown system may be fine for a limited e-reserves system, a commercial product may be a better choice for extended services (Figure 2.12). The *Electronic Reserves Clearinghouse* (**http://www.cc.columbia.edu/~rosedale/**) offers a list of commercial products, links to specific e-reserves projects, links to the ARL e-reserves discussion group, and copyright information relating to e-reserves.

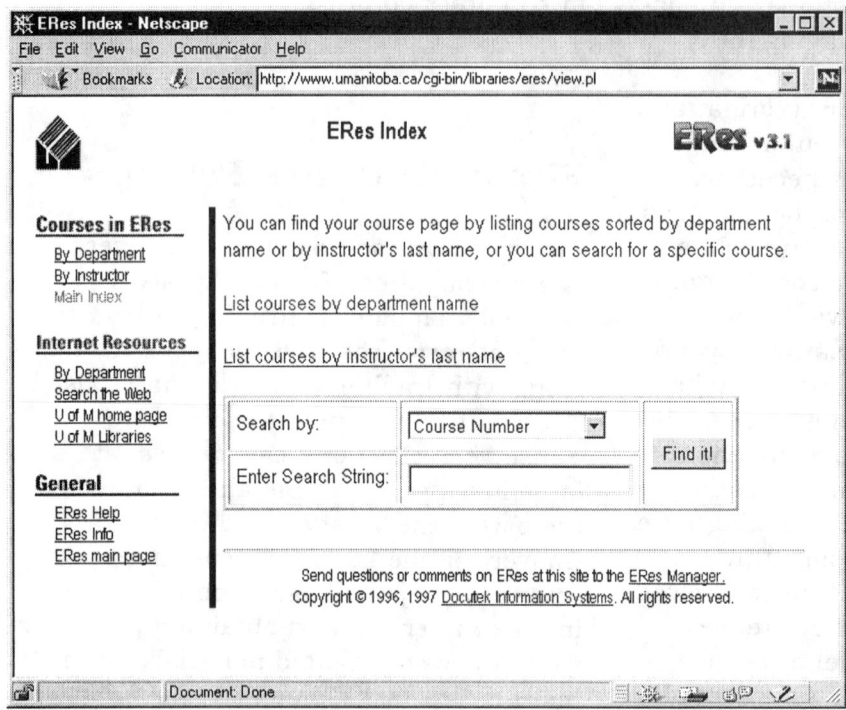

FIGURE 2.12
An e-reserves interface; http://www.umanitoba.ca/cgi-bin/libraries/eres/view.pl

3 The Display of Your Library Web Site

Web pages are unique in the world of information distribution in that the way they display the information they contain and their degree of attractiveness influences both your user's willingness to consider them and the perception of their usefulness. This means that in addition to collecting and organizing the information you consider to be of value to your patrons, you need to put some effort into presenting this information in an appealing way. You also need to make sure it is displayed in a way that makes its information accessible to all of your users.

You may have found that as your patrons have become more familiar with the Web, they have come to expect more in the way of attractiveness and design. This is a new challenge for librarians, and it is exciting to see that more and more librarians are creating web pages that are attractive and engaging. If you look at a wide range of library web pages, as well as other pages on the Web, you will quickly find that manipulating color is one of the most effective and simplest tricks web designers are using to enhance a page's display and attractiveness.

One of the best ways to achieve a pleasing look on the pages in your site is to use your color scheme to tie these various documents together, and wise decisions about color will contribute to a professional looking web site.

Why Using Color Is Important

You will see few web pages anymore that are composed of black text placed against the plain gray background a browser supplies by default. This is because it is easy to incorporate color into your web site by including the HTML coding and the color codes for backgrounds and text within a web page. However, there is more to adding color to your site than just picking some colors that look good and inserting the corresponding tags.

The overarching need for attractiveness means that there should be a rationale for the colors you choose, and you should know that there are other reasons for investing time into this decision. Some of the most important reasons for carefully considering colors are:

To create consistency among your web site pages. In addition to making your web site attractive, you need to create unity among the pages within it. You will find that your site will be composed of many types of informational documents, with many structures and, possibly, in various formats. If you simply transport these resources to your web site by tagging them and linking them together, your site will look disjointed and plain at best. At worst, no one will want to or be able to find the information you have collected.

The types of pages within a library web site can vary greatly. Each department, each resource, even each building of your library may have a different set of resources. You may be including resources intended for different age levels—from children to young adults to adults. You may be designing whole sections of resources for topical areas in which you have found that your users have a frequent interest—business resources, genealogy resources, or best-seller lists are a few such areas. You may have a very focused group of patrons who want all possible variations and formats of their specialized information. As you begin to create a unified set of pages for all of the needs you want to meet, the use of color can be one way to create a relationship between these disparate pages (Figure 3.1).

Thoughtful use of color can be the key that binds web pages together into a cohesive site.

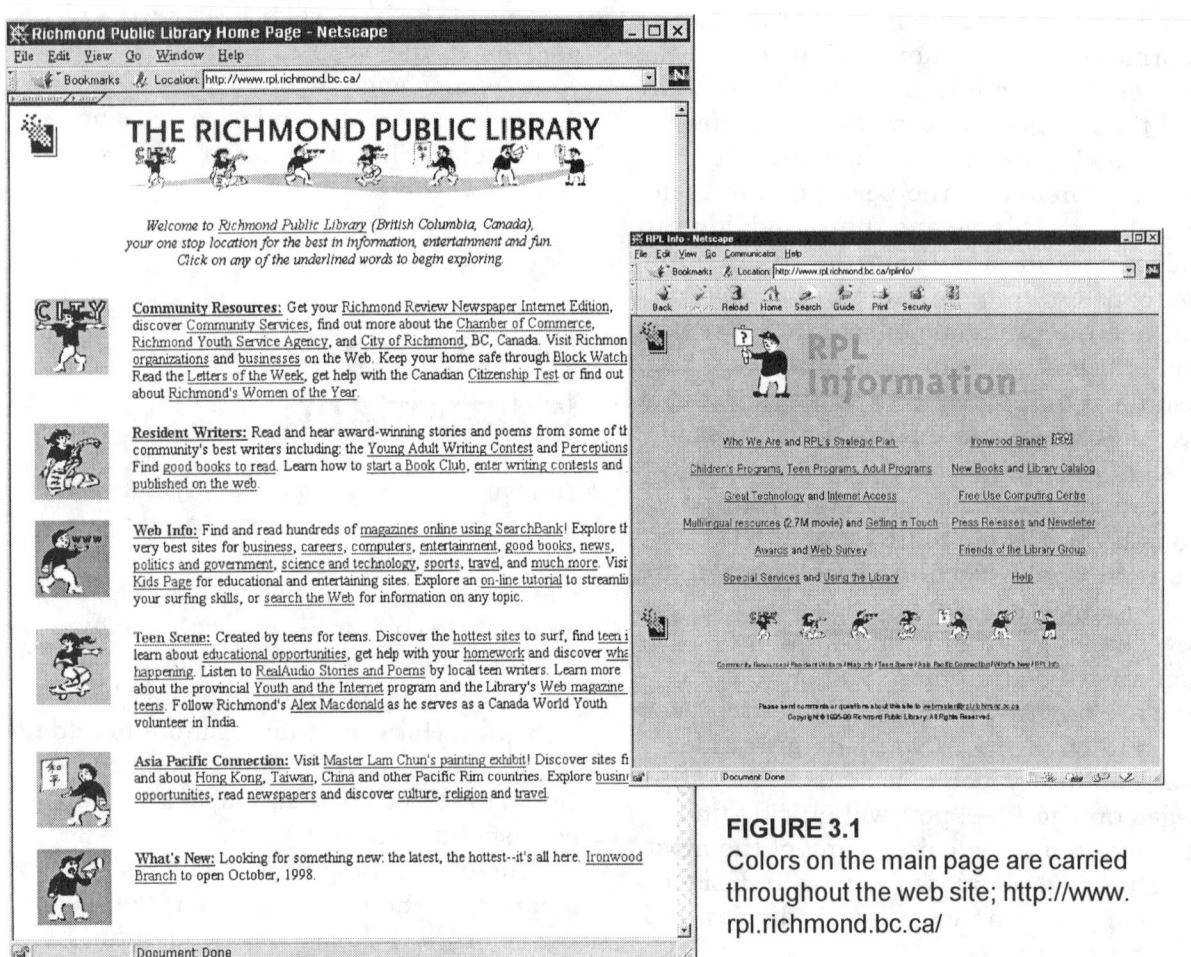

FIGURE 3.1
Colors on the main page are carried throughout the web site; http://www.rpl.richmond.bc.ca/

To get your web site noticed. The appealing use of color can be the main reason one web page will be read and another ignored. People will read an attractive document even if it is not one they were originally interested in, and, given a choice between a "flashy" page and a basic page presenting the same information, most users will choose the attractive one. Usability studies such as the ones we cited in the first chapter tend to corroborate this theory. So you will find that the judicious use of colors can lay the foundation for a web page that is visited often (Figure 3.2).

To differentiate types of information. Bright blue hyperlinks have always been a signal for action on web pages, but other colors can now be used in place of the default blue. You may want to change link colors in order to differentiate between types of hyperlinks, to make text stand out, or to make the contrast of hyperlinks fit in better with the overall page design (Figure 3.3). In addition, it is good to know that the natural tendency of a reader is to give phrases in contrasting color more weight, so the use of color in text can be a powerful tool for highlighting the information to which you want to lead your user.

If you do modify link colors, one thing you will want to avoid is reversing the default colors that most browsers provide; that is, the bright blue for links and purple

FIGURE 3.2
A simple, yet colorful main page;
http://www.tiffinsen.lib.oh.us/

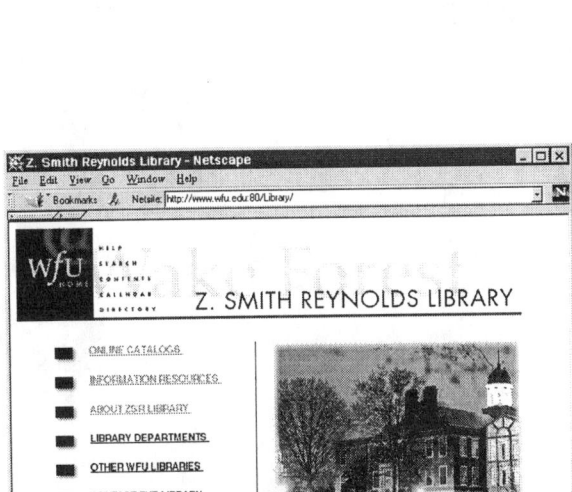

FIGURE 3.3
Link colors may be tailored to match the color scheme of a graphic;
http://www.wfu.edu:80/Library/

for visited links. Reversing this so that purple becomes the unvisited link and blue the visited can be very confusing!

To set the tone of your web site. The tone of your page affects the overall impression a user gets when visiting, and you need to consider the impressions of both the first-time user and the repeat visitor. As you begin to consciously think about creating a tone for your page, you once again need to analyze the needs of your audience. Consider the age, technical ability, educational status, and any other domi-nant characteristics of your primary pa-trons as you experiment with color schemes.

For example, you have probably seen children's pages designed with a color scheme emphasizing bright, primary colors (Figure 3.4). This color scheme can be perfect if its intended audience is young children, but the resulting tone would probably be inappropriate for pages in-tended for young adults, college students, adults, or scholars.

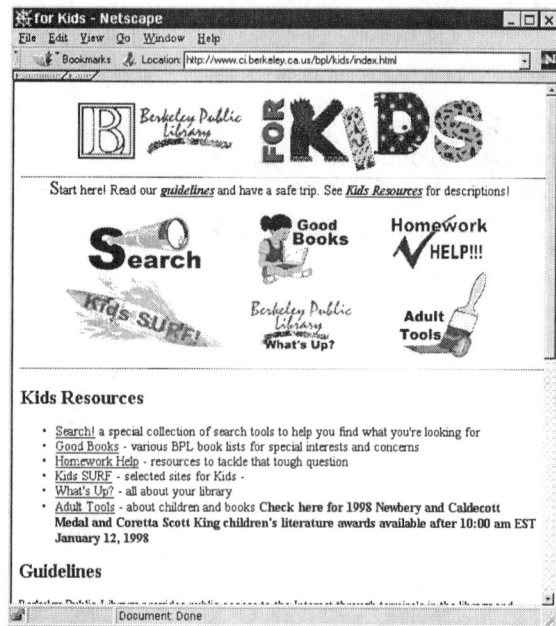

FIGURE 3.4

Two children's pages in primary colors;
http://www.ci.berkeley.ca.us/bpl/kids/index.html,
http://www.cruzio.com/~sclibs/kids/kids.html

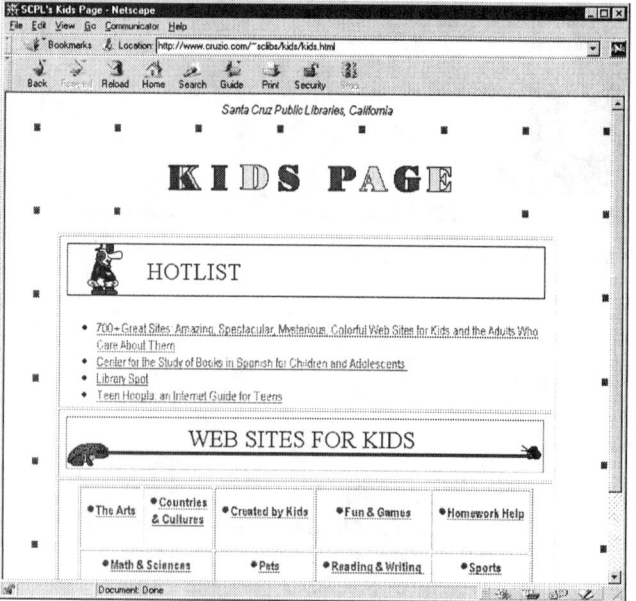

In support of this, Patrick Jones, in "A Cyber-Room of Their Own: How Libraries Use Web Pages to Attract Young Adults" (**http://members.aol.com/naughyde/ virtual.htm**), looked at pages being developed for the young adult (YA) patrons of public libraries. He wanted to know if the principles that have been well-established in the design of physical YA space in public libraries were being carried over into their cyberspace counterparts. The principles he cites reflect the need to distinguish YA areas from others by clearly defining scope, audience, appearance, and collection.

With regard to appearance, Jones found that encouraging young adult participation in the creation of the sites led to the best web page designs, and that "graphics make or break a page: good, age-appropriate graphics make the page attractive to look at, while ugly or childlike graphics, will limit use" (Figure 3.5). This conclusion reinforces the need to create a tone appropriate for your intended audience and to include design elements that will appeal to them (Figure 3.6). It also emphasizes the benefits of including audience feedback in your initial efforts.

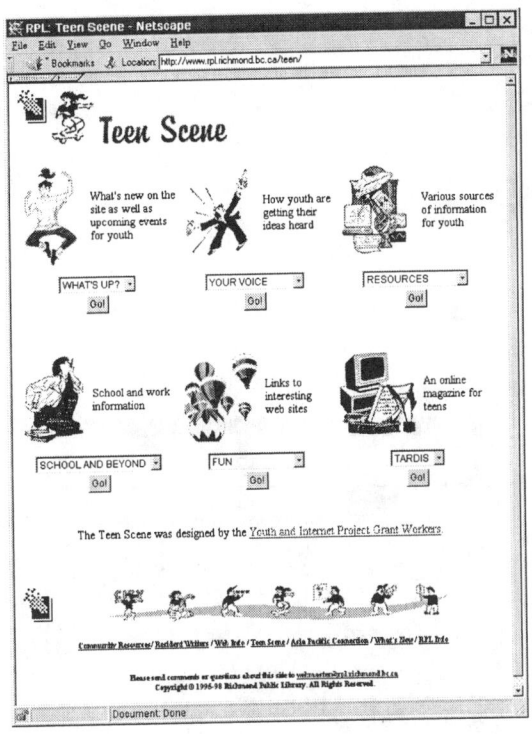

FIGURE 3.5

Age-appropriate graphics are important for young adult sites; http://www.rpl.richmond. bc.ca/teen/

FIGURE 3.6

Color and graphics may be used to support the web site theme; http://www. multnomah.lib.or.us/lib/outer/index.html

The same principle of design holds true for other audiences as well. A scholarly audience might prefer muted colors in a classical design scheme. The JSTOR color scheme, for example, was deliberately chosen to reflect an element of scholarly tradition (Figure 3.7). This decision led to a more sedate color scheme than perhaps an effort to achieve a "high-tech" look would have.

To create an emotional response to your site. You will want your users to "connect" to your site and remember it. One way you can control the response your audience has to your site is by the consistent use of colors and design throughout the separate pages. Information that is displayed with colors and layout that set an appropriate tone will be more memorable than information displayed against a plain background (Figure 3.8).

As you consider the use of color in your web site, remember that color contributes much to the appeal and the overall professional look of your pages. Choosing colors that are appropriate to your audience will

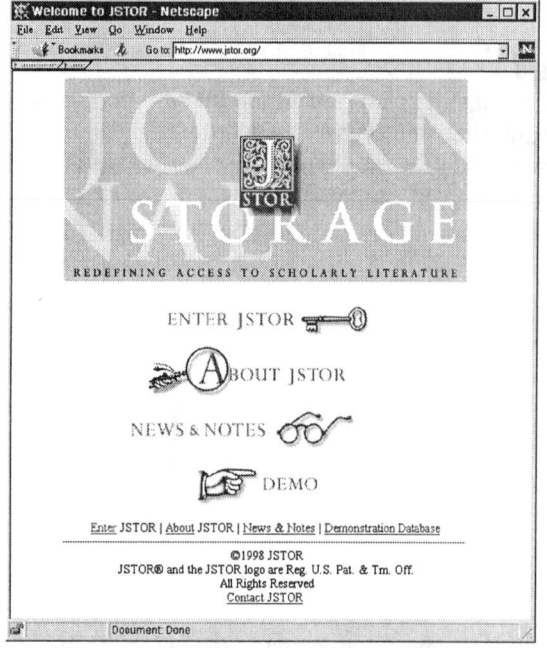

FIGURE 3.7
Traditional colors and design reflect a scholarly environment; http://www.jstor.org/

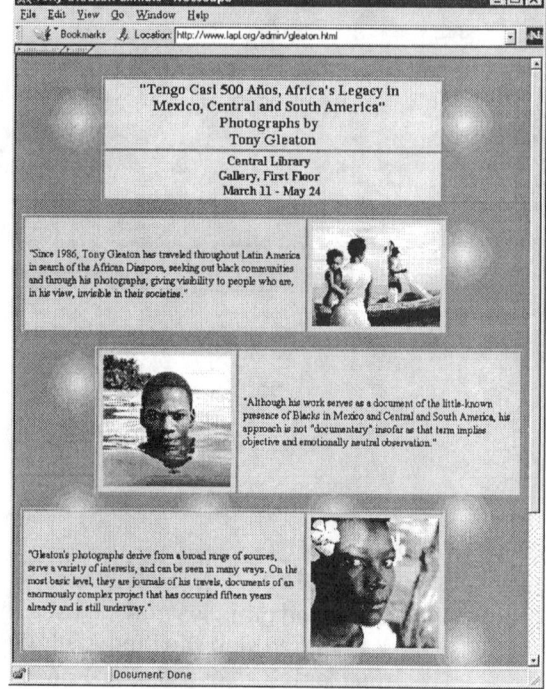

FIGURE 3.8
Colors and graphics may be used to set a specific tone; http://www.lapl.org/admin/gleaton.html

help generate the response you want your audience to have when viewing your pages, and will help ensure that they return.

Plan Your Color Scheme

Since color is so easily placed in a web page, it is very tempting to go overboard as you start experimenting with color combinations. It may be tempting to add lots of background colors with bright links and text, but it is important to remember that only careful coordination and consideration of colors will create an attractive and usable site. Take a look at an array of attractive pages on the Web and you will see that the most pleasing and effective sites use a carefully selected range of colors.

Because color does make such a difference in a site, it is worth taking some time to carefully consider the palette of colors you will want to use in your pages before you start the overall design. As you do this, keep in mind that not only do you want your pages to be attractive and appropriate to your audience, but you also want to ensure that they are physically readable.

As you begin to plan your design and color scheme, take the time to become reacquainted with some elementary color principles. Three basic attributes of color are the *hue*, which is the particular gradation of a color, shade, or tint (or, basically, the name of a color); the *intensity*, or the brightness, of a hue; and the *value* of a color, its degree of lightness or darkness. A hue, or color, with high intensity is very bright. A hue with low intensity is more faded or subdued. A hue with a high value is very dark. For example, consider the color yellow. Yellow is a hue; it can be bright or pale, dark or light.

Different hues can be combined in attractive combinations. For example, complementary primary color combinations are orange and blue, red and green, yellow and purple. For decorative purposes, you really can't go wrong in combining these hues for a basic scheme. For the best consistency in the overall design, you should plan to use the same color intensity in the images and colors you place throughout your pages, making sure that the hues do not clash. The values of colors can be adjusted for various effects. One color of different values can be used for a monochromatic color scheme (Figure 3.9).

Creating contrast between the colors of your web page is extremely important to ensure readability. You need to remember that the color of the text on your pages should not be of the same intensity or close in value to the background color or any background images. The best readability of text is found when there is a great deal of contrast between text and background.

Good combinations of text and background are the standard black on white, dark blue on white, or dark red on white. Colored backgrounds can be a good

FIGURE 3.9
A pleasing monochromatic effect, with highlights; http://www.csbsju.edu/library/

alternative to plain gray or white if the colors are low in intensity. Pastels and pale earth tones with dark text also work well.

One site that offers helpful information about color combinations is *A Palette of Background Colors with Options for Link and Text Colors*, presented by Webspinners (**http://www.spunwebs.com/ bgcolorf.html**). This site enables you to see different colored text presented on a background, making it obvious which color option results in the most contrast and is easier to read.

If you are feeling adventurous, it can be acceptable to create a readable reverse effect by putting light text on a very dark background (Figure 3.10). Remember, though, that if it is a page with content that is likely to be printed, this might cause some problems if the text is white. If you try to print a page with white text against a black background on a printer set to print in grayscale, for example, no text will appear on the printed page.

Combinations like magenta on black, or neon green against neon orange should be avoided. There is simply not enough

FIGURE 3.10
An attractive page can be created by using the reverse effect of white text on black background; http://www.mmb.org.gr/

contrast between the intensity of these colors to provide ease of reading. Similarly, any dark color on a dark background where the values of the colors are equal will not provide adequate contrast.

Another thing to keep in mind is that a certain percentage of the population is affected by color blindness. Eight percent of men and .5% of women may have difficulty reading certain color combinations (**http://www.prevent-blindness.org/ eye_problems/colorvision.html**). This most often occurs with hues of reds and greens, especially if the red and green are of equal intensity. This means that in order for your pages to be viewed by this population, you should try to avoid such color combinations as red text on a green background or vice versa.

A basic principle of color in the print world is that a reader's eyes will go to the outstanding color on a page. If color is clustered in one place, that is where a reader will look first. This holds true for web pages as well, so unless you do have a central spot that you want your users to focus on, try to balance the use of color throughout your page (Figure 3.11). For the same reason, you do not want to blanket *everything* in color. Save it for the information or links you really want to highlight. Within the text blocks of a web page, a single color combined with black is the most effective way to make information stand out.

Another principle to remember is that a black background or border makes colors appear more intense, while colors that are placed next to white look brighter and lighter. This is because the color and brightness of surrounding colors play a role in how other colors are perceived. This fact should affect your choice of backgrounds and borders.

FIGURE 3.11
A balanced effect may be achieved by distributing color on the page; http://www. city.palo-alto.ca.us/palo/city/library/ welcome.html

It can also be helpful to develop an understanding of how colors affect people. Very bright, highly intense yellow, for example, is fatiguing for the eyes and when used as a background on a page will probably annoy those who attempt a sustained reading. Red generates excitement and energy, but can also be tiring in high doses. Light blues and greens are generally calming and, as we mentioned earlier, provide backgrounds that can contribute to easy reading when combined with dark text. If you do choose to use bright colors in your pages, remember to use them sparingly as they can have an overpowering effect. Used minimally as highlights, though, they can be very effective.

Monitors and Browsers

No matter how carefully you create your color scheme, there is the possibility that colors will display differently for your individual patrons. This can be due to variations in monitors, operating systems, or browsers.

The type of monitor one is using plays a part in how colors are displayed. To understand why this is, it can be helpful to know something about how monitors work. Everything on a computer monitor—text or graphics—shows up in pixels. A pixel is a minute square that can only show one color. All colors displayed in the pixels on a monitor are created from combinations of various percentages of red, green, and blue (thus the term RGB color). Black, for example, is achieved by setting the level of all three colors to zero; white by setting them all to their highest level.

Mathematically, there are approximately 16 million possible color combinations in the RGB scheme. Practically, however, not all monitors have the capability for displaying this many colors. Newer monitors that do have the ability to display all the pos-

sible colors may state that they display "millions of colors," "true color," or "24-bit color." Monitors that display 256 colors, or "hundreds" of colors, are fairly standard in libraries, and many still have PCs connected to monitors limited to 16 colors. You can check the monitor settings of the computers in your library to get an idea of what the standard is. If there are monitors available with different display capabilities, you can check your web pages on them to see the difference in color display.

Differences in display can also vary between operating systems. Colors tend to look darker on a PC monitor than on a Macintosh monitor, although the contrast between colors will be the same. And even though a Macintosh monitor and a PC monitor may both display 256 colors, only 216 of these are the same; the remaining 40 will vary.

The two most commonly used browsers, Netscape and Internet Explorer, take this into account by using only the 216 colors that are common to the Macintosh and Windows operating systems in their display. Therefore, only these 216 colors will display consistently on your web page. So, even though you have a monitor that displays millions of colors, only 216 will display consistently in a web browser. If you have ever seen images or background colors on the Web that look pixelated or blotchy, it is probably because they contain colors other than the 216 colors recognized by browsers.

There are many sources of in-depth information available about monitor color display and color on the Web. The *Yale C/AIM Web Style Guide* (**http://info.med. yale.edu/caim/manual/graphics/ display_primer.html**) has a section that explains basic terminology and some of the technical aspects of the differences between monitors.

A respected source of information on color display is Lynda Weinman (**http:// www.lynda.com**), who has authored many books and done a geat deal of work in the field of web color and advanced graphics. Weinman was the original creator of the "browser-safe palette," as she has termed it, a color palette consisting of the 216 colors that display consistently on a browser. She has made this palette available on her web site. You can find it in other places as well, as it has become a widely accepted tool for web designers. Choosing colors from the browser-safe palette will help guarantee that the color you think you are including will show up consistently on everyone's screen. Weinman's web site also contains good explanations of the way color works on the Web and provides links to many excellent color resources.

Another helpful site to visit to learn about color on the Web is the color tools page provided by the Vision Team at **http://www.visionteam.com/color/color.html** (Figure 3.12). They provide some attractive color combinations of text and background, links to color resources, and general tips for designing with color, including reminders such as "No more than four colors per site. Pick from the magic 216."

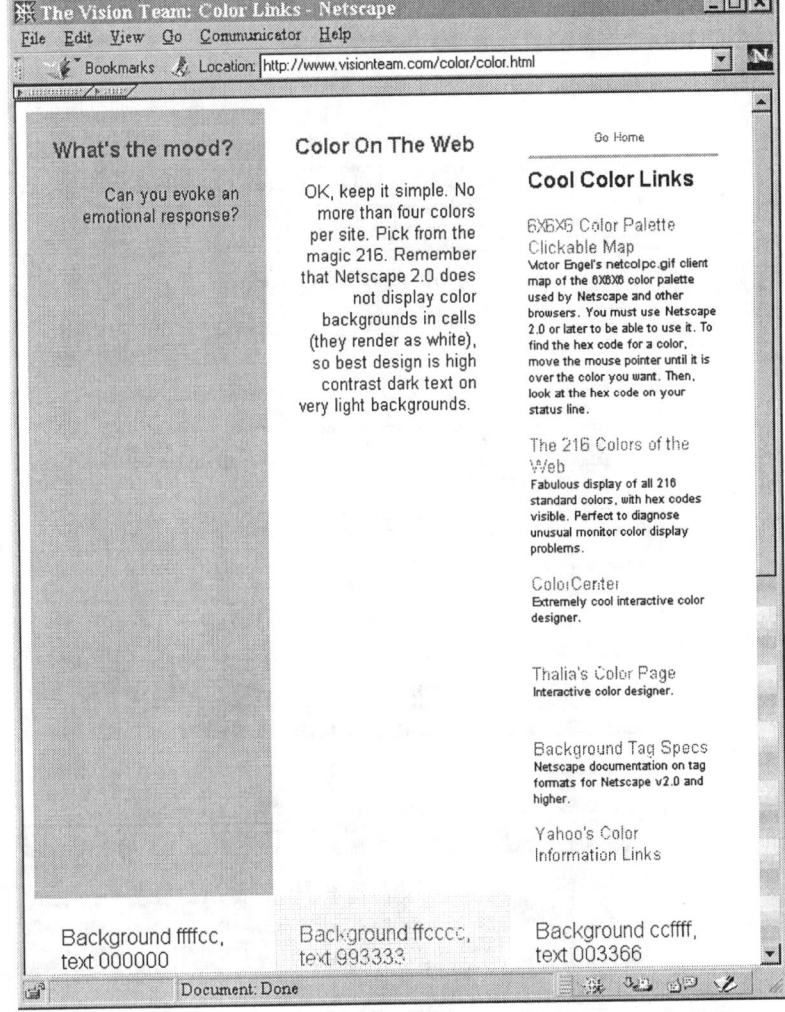

FIGURE 3.12
The Vision Team site provides links to many color resources; http://www.visionteam.com/color/color.html

How to Use Color in Your Pages

Once you have selected colors that will work for your site, adding them to your web page can be done very easily by including some special HTML tagging. These tags can be applied to backgrounds, links, text, portions of text, and even cells or rows within a table. These tags are, again, based on the RGB values: varying percentages of the three primary colors of red, green, and blue. HTML color tags are expressed in *hexidecimal* codes, which means there are six characters (all taken from the character set of 0–9, A–F) representing RGB values. As you might guess, the first two characters represent the percentage of red, the second pair represents the percentage of green, and the last two, blue. For example, black is represented by #000000 (the equivalent of setting all RGB values to 0); white by #FFFFFF (the equivalent of setting all three values to their highest level).

Even though you could theoretically create codes for any of the 16 million possible RGB colors, and mathematical formulas do exist for converting RGB values to hexidecimal codes, you need to remember from the previous discussion that only 216 colors will display consistently in browsers. The Netscape site, accordingly, has an online set of hexidecimal codes for the 216 colors that fit into its browser system palette, and it also provides instructions for including the color code tagging in your documents (Figure 3.13).

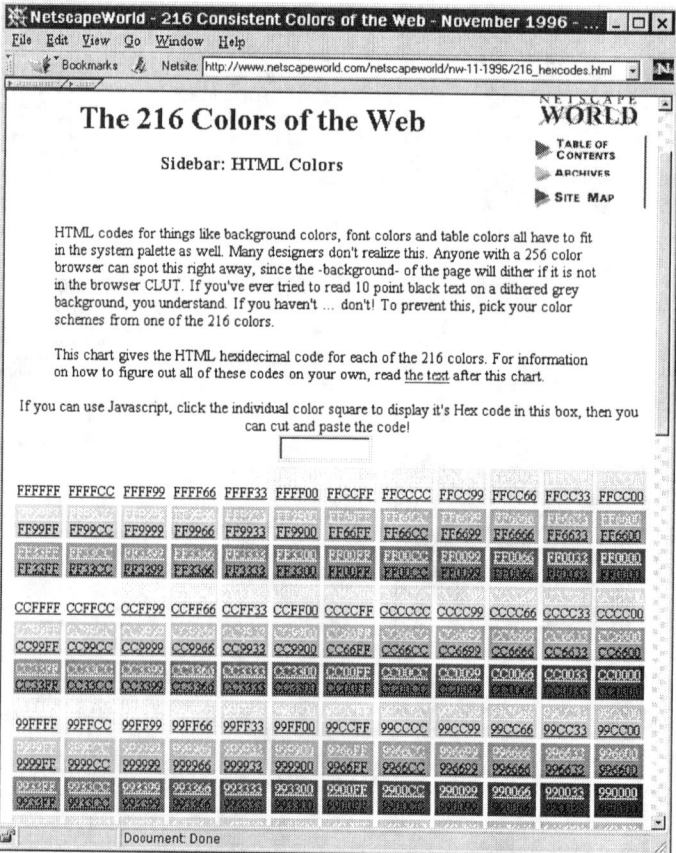

FIGURE 3.13

The Netscape World site demonstrates the 216 colors in the browser palette; http://www.netscapeworld.com/netscapeworld/nw-11-1996/216_hexcodes.html

There are many other online resources that will generate colors and provide the HTML codes for you (Figure 3.14). A fun site for experimenting with color use in backgrounds, text, and links is the ColorCenter. This site changes color automatically as choices for various combinations are made, making it quick and easy to try out different color combinations. The appropriate tagging is displayed for each choice, and this tagging can be copied and pasted into your own web pages.

ColorServe Java is a color generator written especially for use over a modem; so you can use it when you need a color tool that will load quickly. It, too, will present the color combinations you choose in a form that you can include in your tagging.

The newest versions of Internet Explorer and Netscape (3.0 and above) recognize many colors by name, and as these versions become more widely used, that will make adding color even easier. As an example, think of how much easier it is to remember that your background is "Antiquewhite" and your text is "Midnightblue" than remembering "#FAEBD7" and "#191970" as your color scheme combination.

The list of color names is available online in many places. One librarian has created a chart of browser-recognized colors and their names (as well as the

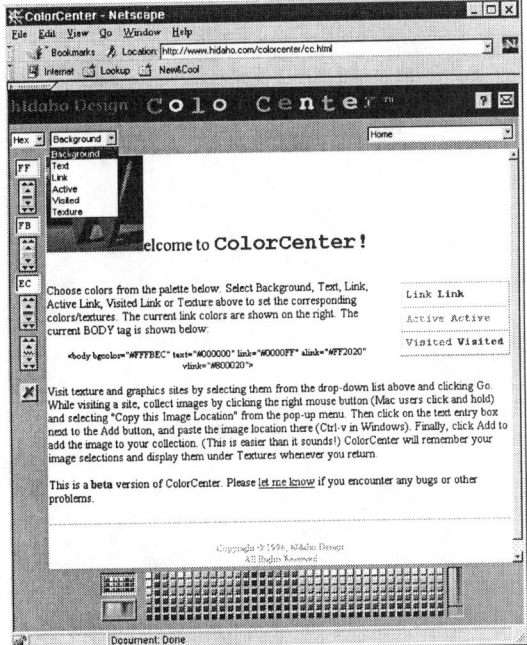

FIGURE 3.14

Many color code generators are available on the Web; http://www.hidaho.com/colorcenter/cc.html, http://www-students.biola.edu/~brian/csapplet.html

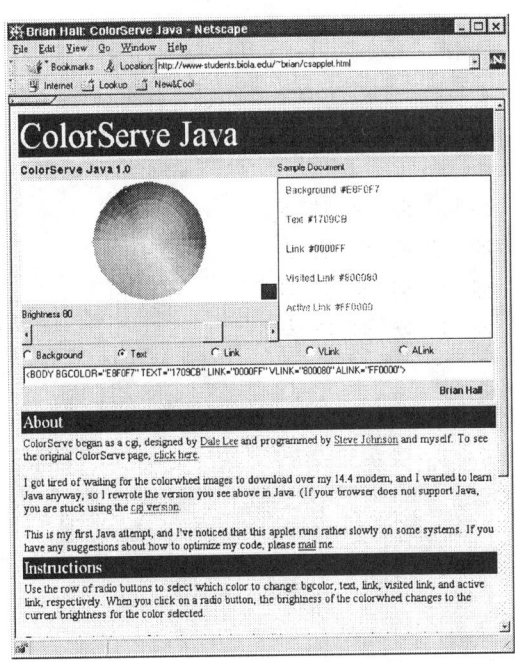

hexidecimal color codes) and provided it online at the SUNY Morrisville Library Links, RGB Color Codes page: **http:// www.morrisville.edu/pages/library/ reference/colorcodes.htmlx**.

These color names are also found in the Netscape site's DevEdge Online Documentation. It can be reached by going to **http://developer.netscape.com/docs/ manuals/htmlguid/** and selecting "Color Units."

It is certainly possible to use background graphics in web pages, but the use of HTML color codes is preferable for several reasons. Using background images is not recommended because:

- Background images take extra time to download.

- A broken-image symbol will appear if a user is viewing your pages with images turned off.

- It is easier on the eyes to place page elements against a plain background than against a complex image.

Including color codes will not add to the download time and will not be as likely to create background noise that is distracting to the reader (Figure 3.15).

Put some thought into the colors you use in your web pages. Careful use of color is one of the most effective ways to create an attractive and unified web site. Remember to consider the appropriateness of your color scheme for your audience, and make sure that your colors allow users to read your pages easily. As you concentrate on making your display work effectively, try to view your pages on as many different monitors and browsers as are available to you. You want to make sure that your display carries through as intended to as many of your users as possible.

FIGURE 3.15
ColorCenter demonstration of textured background— impossible to read;
http://www.hidaho.com/colorcenter/cc.html

4 Library Web Page Layout

We have discussed the ways that display issues can affect the presentation of a web site. It is equally important to create a layout that will present your content in the most appropriate manner. In the past HTML offered little control to the author of a web page. As browser technology and HTML have evolved, though, there are now more ways to control layout, and by far the two most widely used methods for controlling layout are tables and frames.

Tables As Design Tools

Since their introduction, tables have become increasingly relied upon by web page authors. Although Netscape was originally the only browser that was able to display tables, recent versions of Netscape and Internet Explorer display tables almost identically. Even current versions of Lynx are able to display the textual contents of a table if the table has been correctly tagged. This means that tables can safely be used to create desired effects without the worry that some popular browsers might not render them properly.

Tables can be best visualized as being similar to spreadsheets or charts. HTML tags are used to define the rows, columns, and cells within a table. These elements will adjust themselves to fit the content within them, or can be set to predetermined sizes. Other table characteristics, such as the amount of space between borders and content, the space around cells, and the width of borders, can all be adjusted as well (Figure 4.1).

Although the original function of tables was primarily for presenting tabular data, tables immediately became popular as a design feature. Tables are indeed useful for presenting data and charts, but they have come to have other important applications now as well, such as:

- Controlling the width of a page

- Creating columns of text and separating blocks of text

- Aligning images with text and aligning multiple images

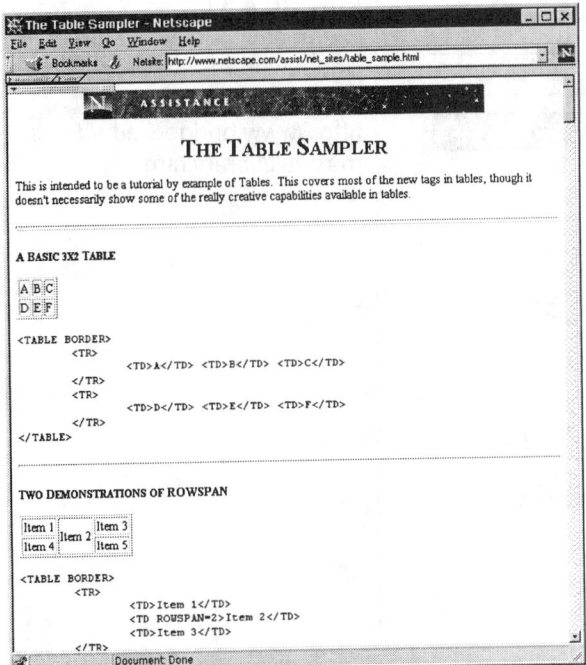

FIGURE 4.1
Netscape page of table diagrams;
http://www.netscape.com/assist/net_sites/
table_sample.html

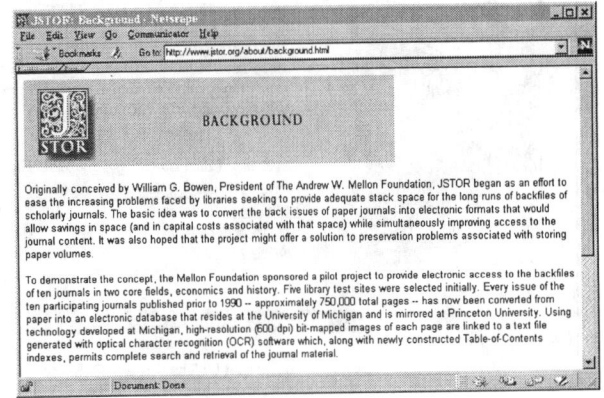

FIGURE 4.2
A web page on a PC window without the use of a table to limit page width; http://www.jstor.org/about/background.html

Controlling the Width of a Page

Why is it important to control the width of a page? Monitor and browser window sizes vary from computer to computer, making it difficult to estimate how to design a web page for all the possible widths of your patrons' browsers. Generally, browser windows on Windows computers will be wider than browser windows on a Macintosh monitor, so graphics that look fine on a Windows machine will be too wide to look good on a Macintosh. Conversely, text that is aligned perfectly on a Macintosh will tend to stretch far to the right across a PC monitor (Figure 4.2).

You will want your library web pages to look alike on as many monitors as possible even though differences in monitor displays exist. You can use tables to control these discrepancies by defining the width of the content on a web page. To do this, you can set a table to a fixed width and place your content within it, basically using the table as a container. The width of a table can be set either in absolute terms by specifying the number of pixels that you would like your content to span, or in relative terms by specifying percentages, which results in tables or columns that will adjust to fit the screen as the browser window is resized.

As a rule of thumb, default browser windows on Macintosh monitors and 14" PC monitors are about 475 to 600 pixels wide, while larger PC monitors will probably pop open browser windows that are much wider. Designing with tables set within the lower range of 475–600 pixels will ensure that the width of the page looks pretty much equal (in actual pixel size) on all monitors (Figure 4.3).

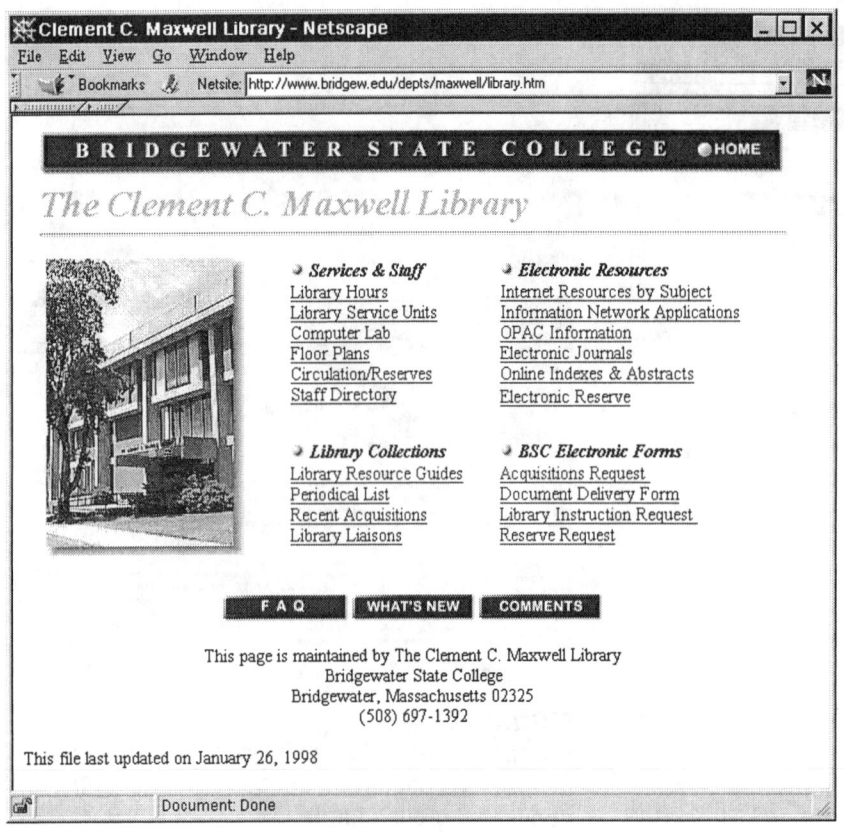

FIGURE 4.3
Clement C. Maxwell Library at Bridgewater State University, table set for 600 pixels; http://www.bridgew.edu/depts/maxwell/library.htm

This is useful if you are using a graphic as a header and want your text to line up to the same width as the header to avoid a lopsided look. To do this, you can put your content within a fixed width table. This will ensure that even if the browser window is adjusted, the width of your content will stay the same.

Designing with the width of the table set to percentages will create pages that look proportionally the same, regardless of the size of the monitor. For example, a table set to a width of 80 percent will always stretch or shrink so that it takes up 80 percent of the width (Figure 4.4).

You will also need to consider how the page will look as it is printed out, keeping in mind the printable area of a page as you set the width of your table. Generally, if you would like a page to fit within the width of piece of 8 ½" x 11" paper, the maximum width of the surrounding table should be set for no more than 535 pixels.

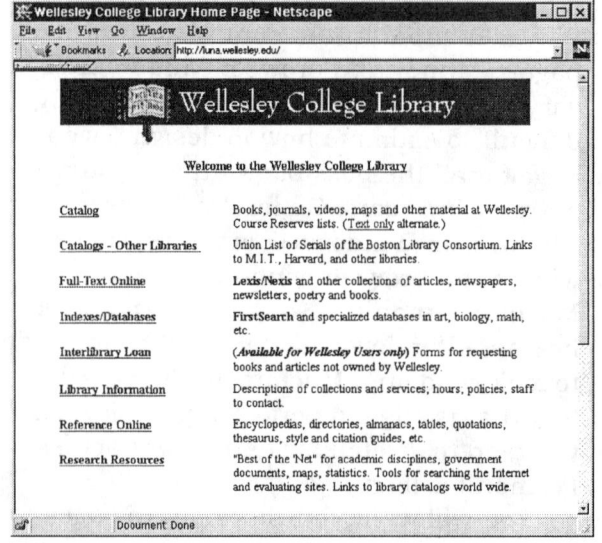

FIGURE 4.4
Wellesley College Library, table set for 80%; http://luna.wellesley.edu/

Creating Columns and Placing Text

Before the use of tables, text pretty much had to run from the farthest left margin of a web page all the way to the right. Long lists of data could be bulleted or numbered, but not really separated into blocks of text that could easily be differentiated for reading. Paragraph tags <p> were the only way to create horizontal space between blocks of text.

Tables can make web page layout much more flexible by allowing you to place text on a page and keep it in one position. Text blocks and other elements can be placed in specified areas on the page (Figure 4.5). Tables can also be used to create newspaper-style columns which break up the text and make it easier to read (Figure 4.6).

This technique allows for a more effective presentation of large amounts of textual information.

It is very important to remember that if patrons in your intended audience might be using a screen reader, they will not be able to read text in columns. Screen readers will read text across a page, not down, and therefore will not present the text in correct order. If you do use tables to create columns of text and you believe that screen readers might be used to access the information in your page, provide an alternatively formatted file for users who need it.

Text in columns can be used to create a textual toolbar along the sides, tops, or bottoms of pages. Tables can also be used to create margins along the right- or left-hand sides of web pages; again, something that was impossible to do before the introduction of tables (Figure 4.7).

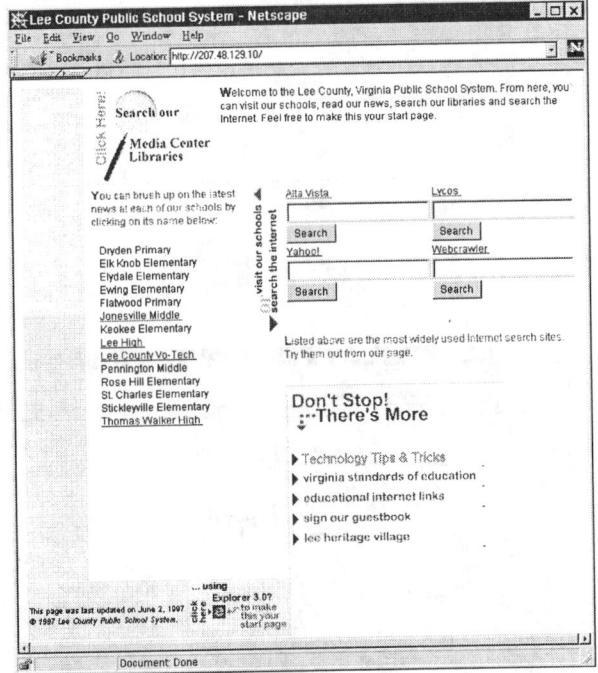

FIGURE 4.5
Lee County Public School System,
placing text blocks in carefully selected areas
for a more controlled layout;
http://207.48.129.10/

FIGURE 4.6
A guide to the Columbia University Libraries,
using tables to break text into columns;
http://www.columbia.edu/cu/libraries/culpubs/
culguide.1996-1997/

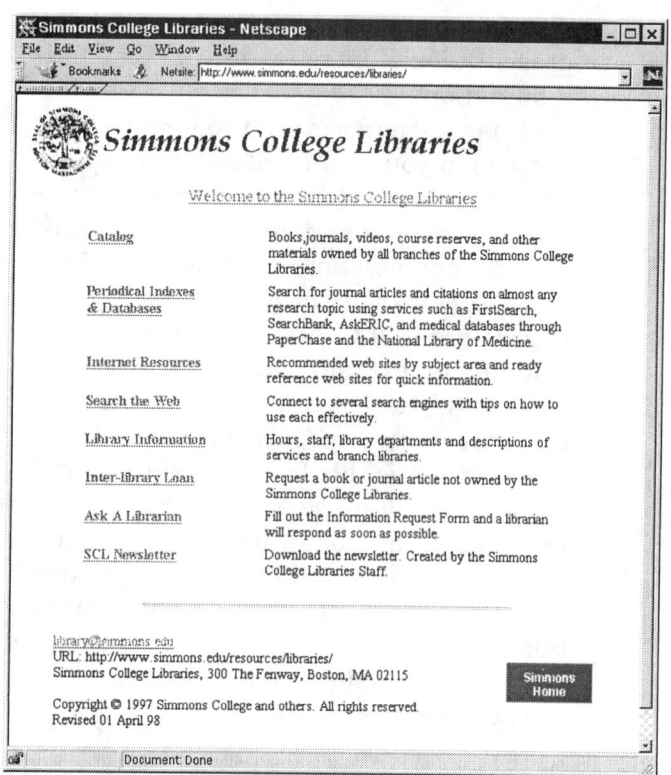

FIGURE 4.7
Simmons College Libraries, text placed in table columns to create margins; http://www.simmons.edu/resources/libraries/

Aligning Images with Text or Aligning Multiple Images

Before tables, it was very difficult to make text wrap around an image correctly and stay in place as a browser window was resized or as it was viewed on different monitors. You can now use table cells to make it easy to place images and text next to each other—text can easily be placed above, below, or to the right or left of an image by choosing an adjoining cell. In addition, if you wish to use it, tables have a built-in caption capability. Captions create a bold header that can be placed above or below cells with images, depending on design needs.

The same method can be used for pages that contain multiple images. Instead of leaving the alignment up to the way the browser displays images, they can be placed within cells on a page and will stay there (Figure 4.8). Images placed within cells of a table with the border set to

FIGURE 4.8
San Diego Public Library, using a table to align images; http://www.sannet.gov/public-library/

zero will appear to have no space between them. This technique, when used to divide large images into smaller ones, can contribute to faster loading of web pages. For example, the first page of the Yale University Library site looks as though it contains one large image when it is actually seven smaller images put together seamlessly in a table (Figure 4.9). These smaller images load more quickly than would one large image.

Some Tips for Using Tables

The use of tables for design purposes will take some experimentation and practice. Some techniques that we have found to be useful may be helpful to you as well:

- Adjust border widths for different effects. Borders set to zero are invisible. Using invisible borders is probably one of the most widely used techniques on the Web. This technique allows you to place text or images anywhere on a page without revealing any separating lines (Figure 4.10). Or you can adjust a table border to display thicker lines in order to create various grid effects (Figure 4.11).

- For pages that require large tables, consider using a series of smaller tables instead for faster loading of pages. Large tables that contain a lot of content will take longer to download.

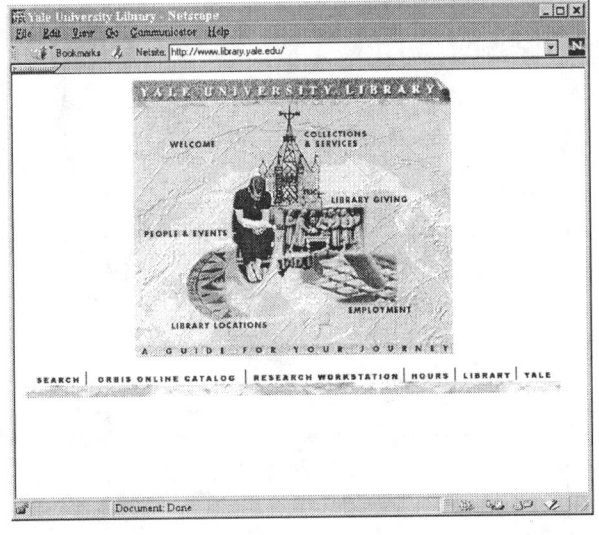

FIGURE 4.9
The main Yale University Library web page features a large image which is actually composed of many small images placed within a table; http://www.library.yale.edu/

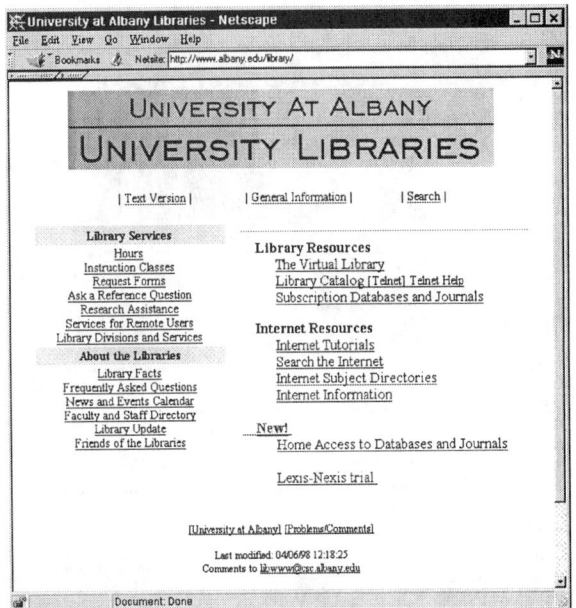

FIGURE 4.10
SUNY Albany, use of a table with invisible borders; http://www.albany.edu/library/

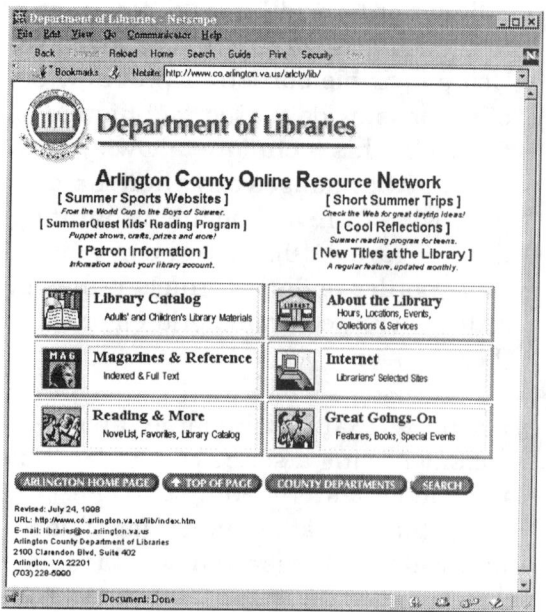

FIGURE 4.11
Arlington County Online Resource Network, table borders used as design elements; http://www.co.arlington.va.us/arlcty/lib/

- Colors can be used in individual cells and columns to add more differentiation to a page. This can be particularly useful for tabular data, where alternating colored rows can help a user view the content without getting lost. Color can also be added to table borders for design purposes (Figures 4.12 and 4.13). A useful online color tool, the ColorPicker by Professional Web Design, places your color choices within a table so you can select colors and see how they will display within cells and rows (**http://junior.apk.net/~jbarta/weblinks/color_picker/**).

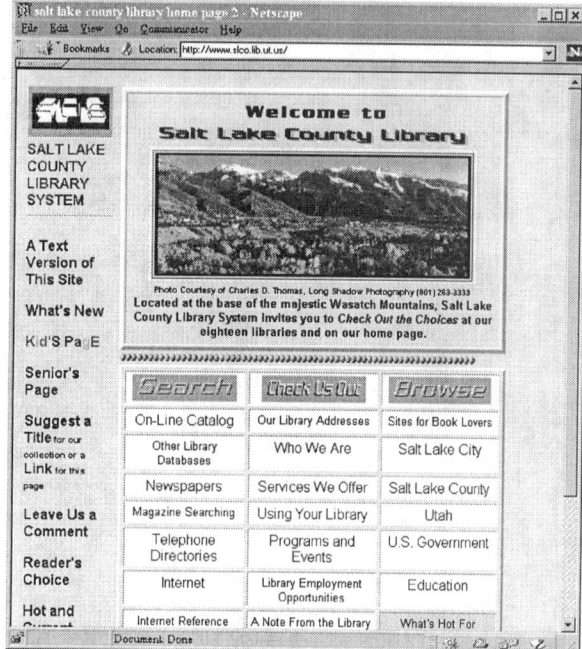

FIGURE 4.12
Salt Lake County Library, tables used for color and alignment; http://www.slco.lib.ut.us/

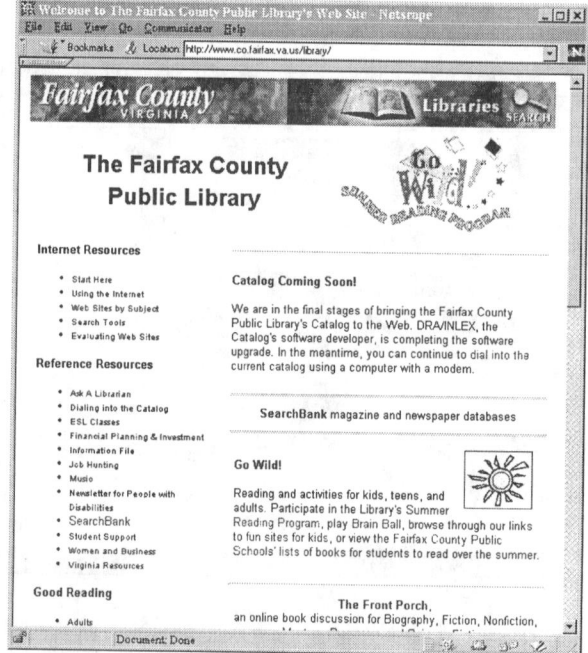

FIGURE 4.13
The Fairfax County Public Library Home Page, color used within table elements; http://www.co.fairfax.va.us/library/

- To make it easier to create a table, think of building your table row by row. If you think of your design in terms of rows, columns, and cells, this will make it much easier to visualize the result.

- Complicated tables should be sketched out before you start tagging, and looking at the sketch as you create your document can make it easier to keep track of the many levels of HTML tags that are used to create the rows, columns, and cells.

- Each time you end a row, you should consider including a line break tag <BR>. This will allow browsers that do not render tables to show the contents of your table with each row's data on a separate line. Even though users of these browsers will not be able to see the actual table layout, this will serve to separate your information in the proper places, making it usable and understandable.

- If you have used tables within a document that you expect will be printed out, do a test printing to check the formatting. Sometimes very long columns of text will not print out in their correct order. Columns that are longer than one page will lead the reader of the print version through all subsequent pages and then back to the first page. And if the width of a table has been set too wide, its contents may be outside of the printable margin.

There are many resources available for those who are interested in learning how to create tables. Two basic guides are the Netscape table page (**http://www. netscape.com/assist/net_sites.tables. html**) and *A Beginner's Guide to HTML* section on tables (**http://www.ncsa. uiuc.edu/General/Internet/WWW/ HTMLPrimerP3.html#TA**). These guides offer all the instructional assistance needed to learn the basics of table tagging.

Frames As Design Tools

Frames, like tables, can enhance your options for controlling the layout of a page. Netscape 2.0 and above and Internet Explorer 3.0 and above support frames and, like tables, they are becoming more widely accepted across the Web. Frames make it possible to display multiple HTML documents in a single browser window. Frames can also make it possible to launch multiple browser windows and to control the contents of each window through hyperlinks set in other windows. The page designer controls the size, number, and destination of each of the individual framed documents on the screen.

A frame can best be thought of as an area statically positioned within a web page that contains an individual HTML document. The main web page is structured as a frameset and may include several frames. Each framed area within the frameset will usually display a different HTML document. Typically, there will be one main framed area that is intended to be the focus of attention. For example, the JSTOR search screen includes three frames. The search form is in the main framed area; the two smaller frames are for the navigational buttons and the copyright statement (Figure 4.14).

It is important to remember that not all web pages are candidates for a frame-style presentation, and the use of frames should be very selective. Frames can be even more complicated to design than tables and they really are appropriate in only a few situations. These situations include the presentation of:

- Constant informational elements

- Navigational choices

- Tables of contents

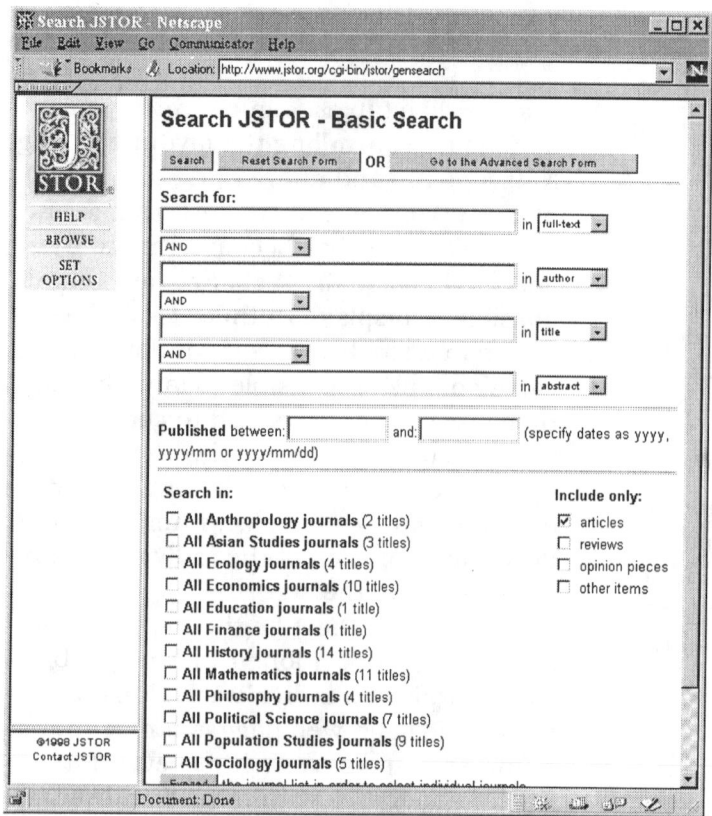

FIGURE 4.14
The JSTOR search page is composed of an overall frameset which includes a main window and smaller windows for navigation and copyright information; http://www.jstor.org/cgi-bin/jstor/gensearch

Presenting Constant Informational Elements

It is possible to change one frame window while another remains static, so some informational elements can stay on a user's screen without being redrawn as links are selected. Such elements as copyright notices, logos, or contact information can be fixed in a static, individual frame that becomes a consistent part of every page (Figure 4.15). Time can be saved each time a new hyperlink is selected because these particular frame elements do not need to be downloaded from the server each time a new page is retrieved.

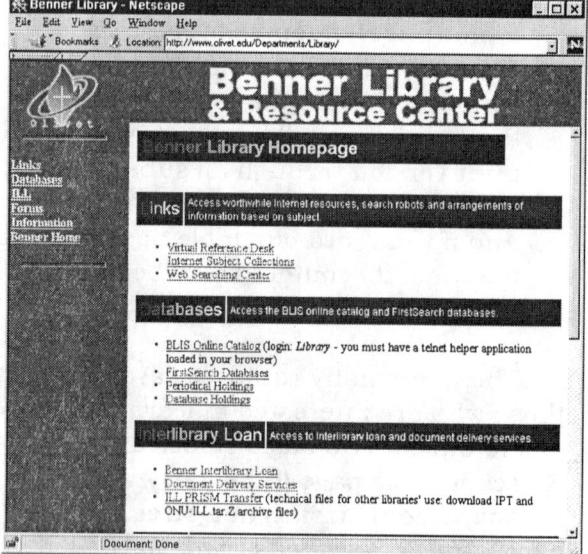

FIGURE 4.15
Olivet Nazarene University's Benner Library and Resource Center; the bands across the top and to the left are actually separate framed documents; http://www.olivet.edu/Departments/Library/

Presenting Navigational Choices

On framed web sites, hyperlinks in one frame can be used to update the content of adjacent frames, making it possible, with thoughtful layout and planning, to provide an intuitive navigation interface to your web site (Figure 4.16). Frames can be especially useful if there are navigational or directional choices that vary with specific pages within a site. For example, it is possible to place a table of contents or toolbars in a frame adjoining the main content window. These choices can change as the context of the main document changes. For example, in the JSTOR interface, navigation buttons in the left frame present options that relate to the content of the main frame. If one is viewing a table of contents, the options are different than those presented when one has reached the point of printing.

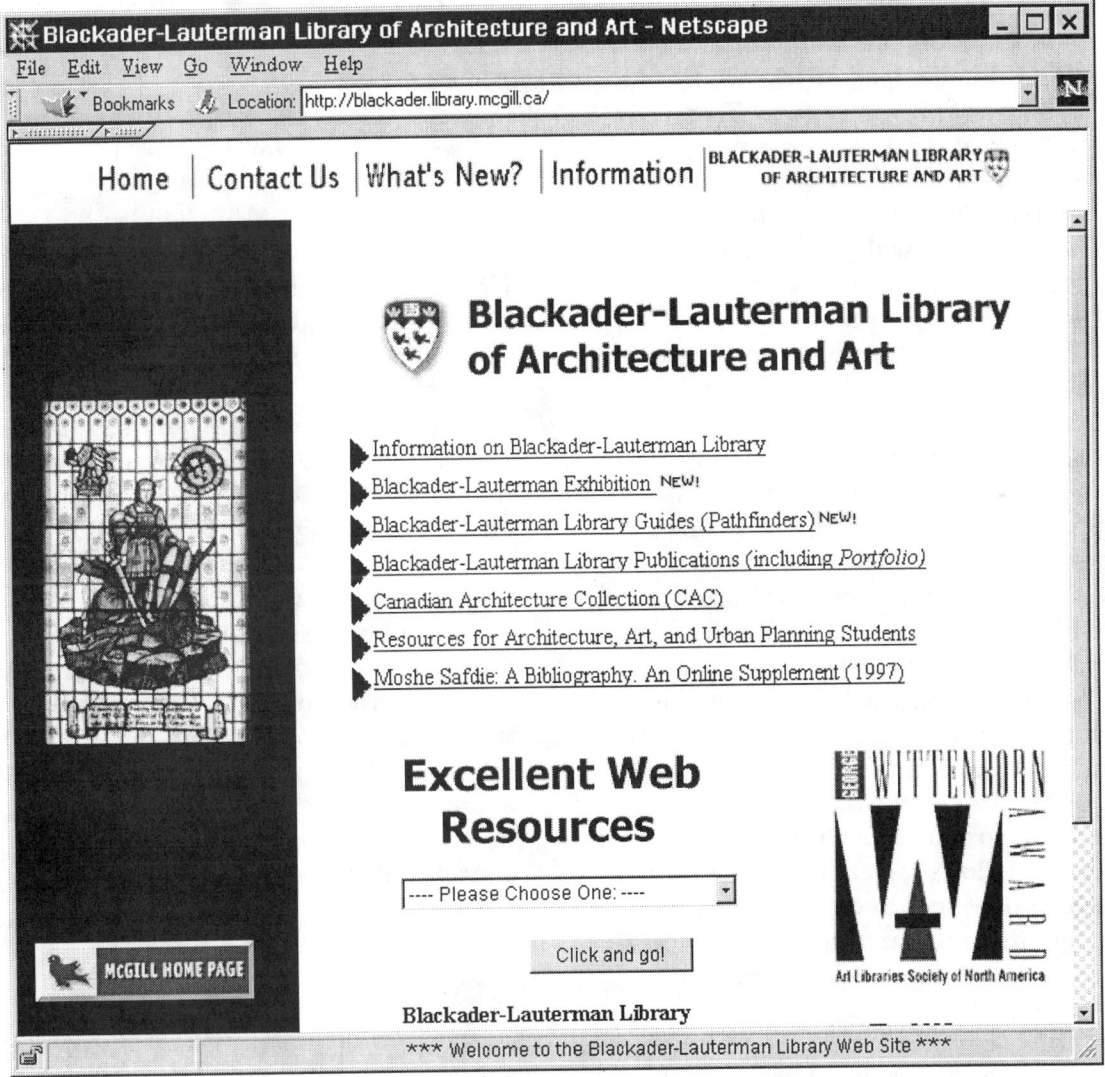

FIGURE 4.16
Blackader-Lauterman Library presents navigational options in the topmost frame of its web page; http://blackader.library.mcgill.ca/

Presenting Tables of Contents

Frames can be used to provide a table of contents or index for your web site. By allowing your users to have a constant reminder of selectable options, they will always be reminded of the information you have collected in your site. For example, the Hennepin County Library keeps a table of contents in a frame to the left of all its pages (Figure 4.17).

Some Tips for Using Frames

Be aware of the problems that can arise when using framed pages. If you are not careful in setting up hyperlinks within your individual framed HTML documents, pages within your site will not always follow the common navigational behavior that users have come to expect with nonframed web pages. This can lead to confusion. Test your framed web pages to make sure that the "back," "forward," and "reload" buttons of a browser work as your users expect them to.

Printing a framed page is also not as straightforward as printing a nonframed web page as browsers handle printing of framed pages differently. Some versions of browsers will print the entire screen as displayed on a monitor; some will print only the main frame. Often if a user has unknowingly selected or clicked on a frame, that HTML document will be the only one that will print out.

Framed pages can take a long time to load. If there are many windows in a page, and each one contains a separate HTML document, it follows logically that this will increase the time required to load the entire page. Keep this in mind if your users tend to be connecting via slow connections, such as a modem.

With these caveats in mind, and knowing that there are times when frames can be a good design solution, here are some tips that we have found useful when working with frames:

FIGURE 4.17
The Hennepin County Library uses frames in its online newsletter; http://www.hennepin.lib. mn.us/library/index_ei.html

- If you are thinking about using a frame simply for layout purposes, consider the use of a table instead. Tables are often more straightforward to work with. If you are unsure whether to use a table or a frame, take the time to do a mockup of each and look for the advantages and disadvantages of each method.

- If there is a possibility that your audience will be using older versions of browsers or text-only browsers, include an alternative to frames by using the "noframes" option. Placing the <noframes>...</noframes> tags around a standard HTML document will allow users of these browsers to see your content, albeit without the framed layout.

- Design the individual documents of a framed page with their ultimate placement in mind. For example, if an HTML document is going to be sharing space with other framed documents in a web page, don't put a wide header in it. Doing so will make it look squeezed in.

- Estimate the size of each framed area carefully. Watch out for scrollbars that will appear if the size of a frame is incorrectly estimated and not consistent with the size of the content. If scrollbars appear within a small framed window, they may obscure it entirely. If you think this might be a problem, there is a tag that will prevent scrollbars from appearing, but if you include it, users might not be able to view all the information in that frame.

- Plan navigation carefully when incorporating frames. As a general rule, do not link to an external site in a way that presents it within one window of your framed page. This will begin a cycle of links to pages within a small window, needlessly miniaturizing the content.

- You can set frames to open to a new window for simultaneous viewing of pages and to make it easier to go back to an originating screen. Do not overuse this technique, though, as too many open browser windows can be confusing. It is important when you do this to let your users know when they are in a different window. On smaller monitors a new window tends to obscure the first, and many people may not realize that a second window has opened (Figure 4.18).

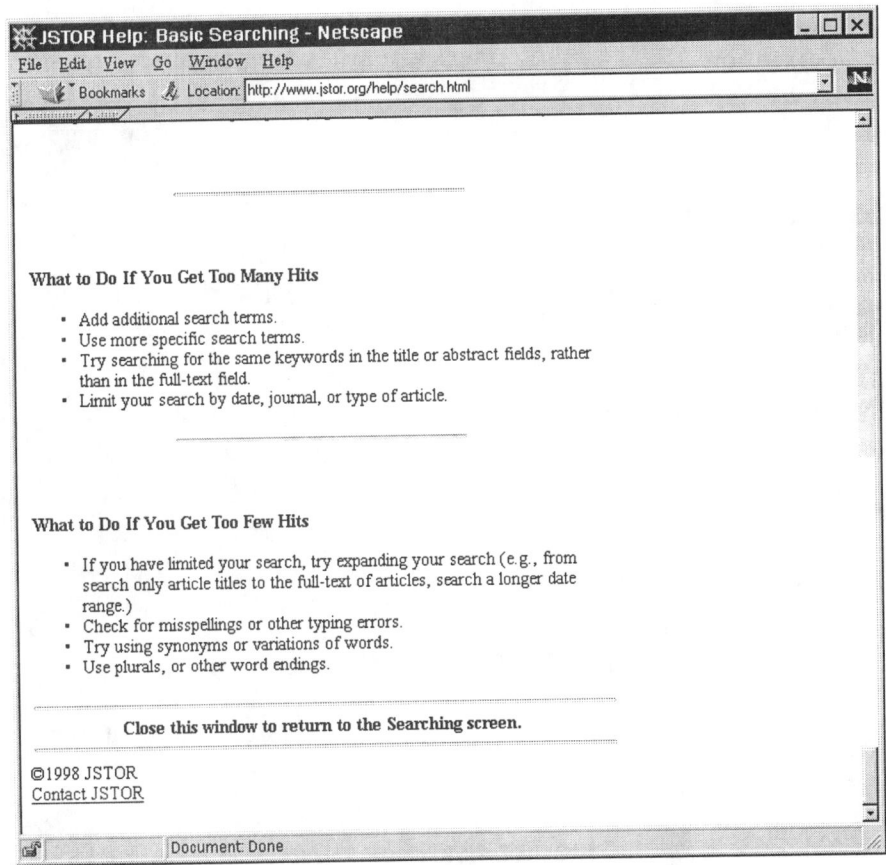

FIGURE 4.18
A JSTOR help screen with a note to close the window to return to the original screen; http://www.jstor.org/help/search.html

Use frames sparingly and only when you are sure that they closely fit your users' needs. Because frames are so complex, sketching out a design and carefully thinking about navigation before beginning is essential. It is also helpful to have references on hand when creating frames. The *Netscape Frame Site* (**http://www. netscape.com/assist/net_sites/frames. html**) is one helpful source that you can refer to as you create framed pages.

Navigation

Using advanced layout options such as tables and frames can make navigation very complex for your users. This risk increases with the size of your web site. As your site grows, you have to take responsibility for providing consistent navigational elements to give your user information about the way your site is organized.

One of the most important things you need to do to make navigation easier is provide context for your users. Your web pages need to include explicit, visual clues about their relationship to other pages in your site. On any given page within your site, users should know where they are in relation to all the other pages you have (Figure 4.19). Even though you may think the relationship of your pages is intuitive, it may only be intuitive to you because you have worked so closely on them. The structure of your site may not be at all apparent to someone visiting your pages. Do not assume that your user can guess how your site is organized—lay it out plainly.

As you consider how to plan for navigation throughout your site, remember to include plans not only for navigation between pages but also for navigation between sections of content on long pages. Many users are still using smaller moni-

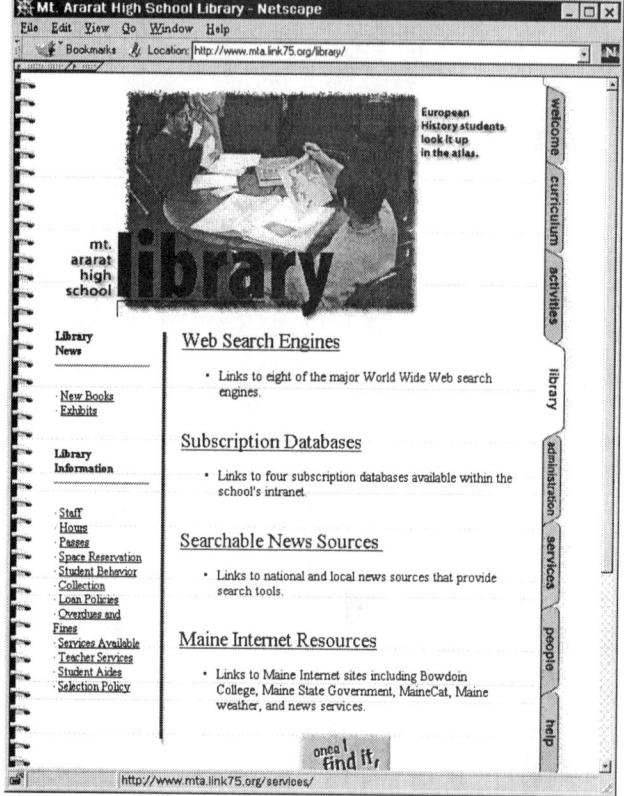

FIGURE 4.19
Mt. Ararat High School incorporates navigational features on its pages which help place the page within the context of the overall site; http://www. mta.link75.org/library/

tors, and a lot of web pages will not fit completely on their screen, making it necessary for them to scroll down to see everything on the page. If you have long pages, and important content falls below what appears on a smaller monitor, include some explicit clues that more information can be found. For example, links at the top of a page can be used to connect to information positioned toward the end of a page.

Navigational Aids

It is possible, depending on the design of your pages, to include a number of aids that will help users navigate through your site. It is important to remember that people have different navigational styles and may prefer one method over another. They also may prefer different methods according to the type of information gathering they are involved in. For example, some people prefer to search, others to browse. Patrons will probably use a searching tool if they are looking for a specific item, but may want to browse if they want an overall sense of what your library site includes. Whether users are searching or browsing, you will want to make sure that they know how to return to specific starting points. Some of the aids you can use to help them are toolbars, pop-up menus, tables of contents, and searching functions.

Toolbars. Toolbars offering navigational choices are widely used on the Web. A toolbar can simply be a list of text options, or it can be composed of one or more images. Graphical toolbars are often integrated into the design of a page, thereby enhancing the look of a site as well as providing navigational choices. If you include graphical toolbars, you need to make sure they *look* like navigational helps, and not just designs. You will also want to include text along with the images. Images used without text to signify instructions can often be misinterpreted. Remember that small images using only a few colors will load most quickly (Figure 4.20). As we have seen, toolbars can be placed in tables or in frames to keep them in a fixed position on your pages (Figure 4.21).

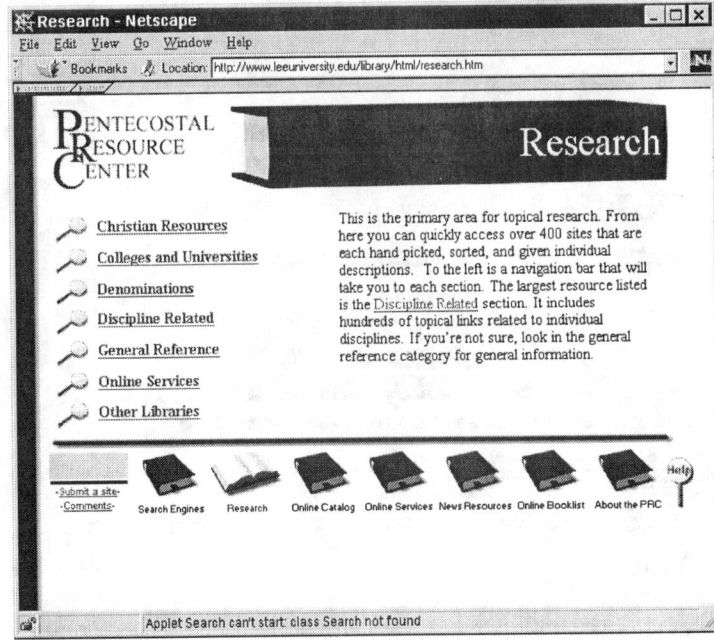

FIGURE 4.20
Lee University Pentecostal Resource Center uses a navigational toolbar composed of small images; http://www.leeuniversity.edu/library/html/research.htm

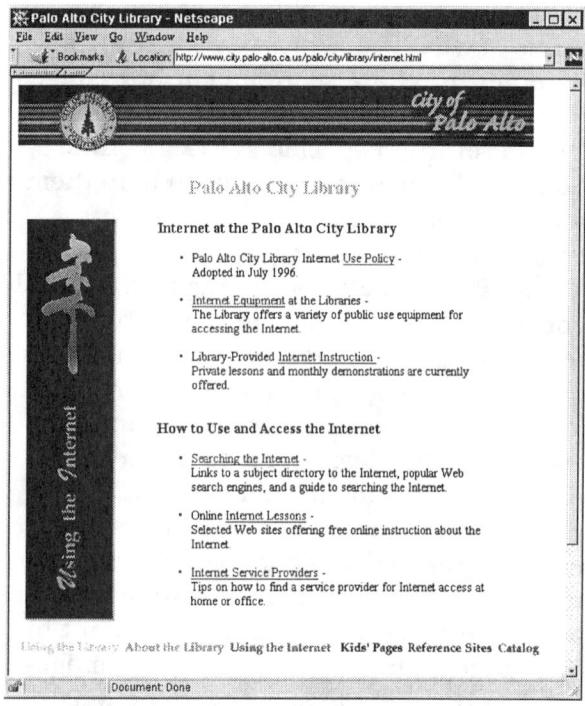

FIGURE 4.21
Palo Alto City Library, toolbars in fixed positions;
http://www.city.palo-alto.ca.us/palo/city/library/
internet.html

There are some navigational fixtures that users tend to look for in every web site. A minimum requirement is that you provide a link to your main page from all pages. However, if you include a toolbar on your pages, you should incorporate into it as many of these options as are found in your site:

- Index   • Home
- Help   • Site map
- E-mail   • Search

Pop-up menus. It is also possible to use forms to lead people through your site. For example, pop-up form menus can be used to compactly list the sections of your web site. These forms can serve two functions: they will allow your user to view a list of the different sections in your site, and they will let them jump immediately to the one they choose. Make sure that your index, or home page, is always listed as one of the choices so that returning to the beginning of your site is never a problem (Figures 4.22a and 4.22b).

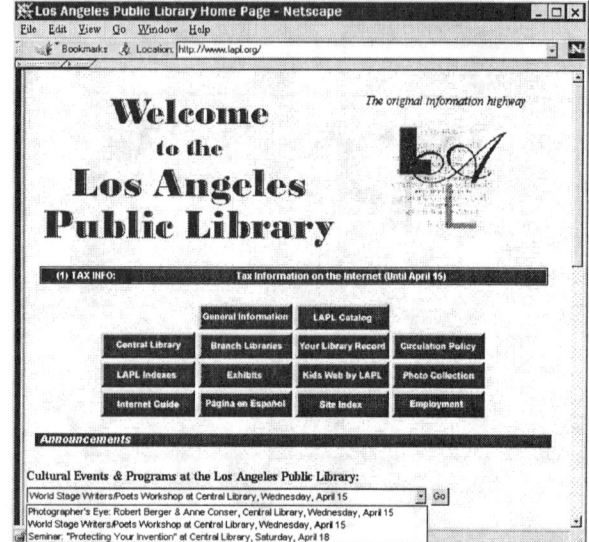

FIGURE 4.22a
Los Angeles Public Library, use of pop-up
menu for navigation; http://www.lapl.org/

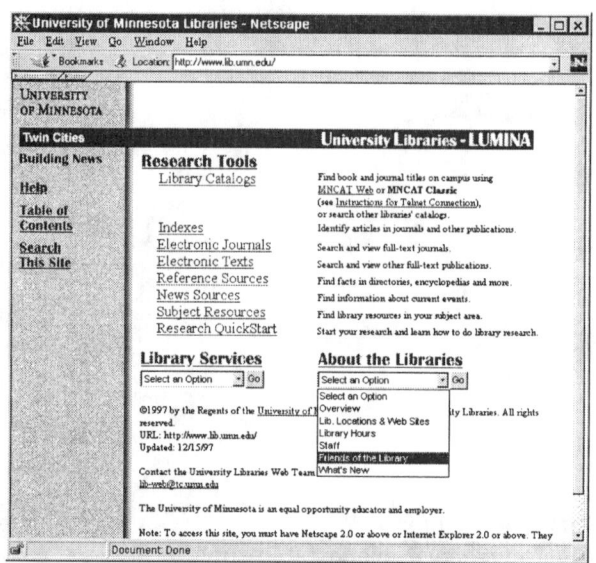

FIGURE 4.22b
University of Minnesota, Twin Cities,
pop-up menus; http://www.lib.umn.edu/

Tables of contents. A table of contents can be helpful to those who would like to view a list of the information you are providing. A table of contents can be as extensive or as general as you like, but a general index is often sufficient. It will not take a lot of updating and will provide helpful context.

Search forms. If you have someone capable of creating a search feature at your library, add searching functions to your web site. Users expect to be able to search large sites for specific information, whether doing research or searching for a particular staff member. You may want to include a search form on the first page of your site, or provide searching functions for specific sections of your web site (Figure 4.23).

When including a search capability in your site, make sure you prominently include some instructions or help files so that your patrons can use this capability effectively. If your site is complex, think about creating a general "tips for navigation" page that incorporates searching help as well as other hints (Figure 4.24).

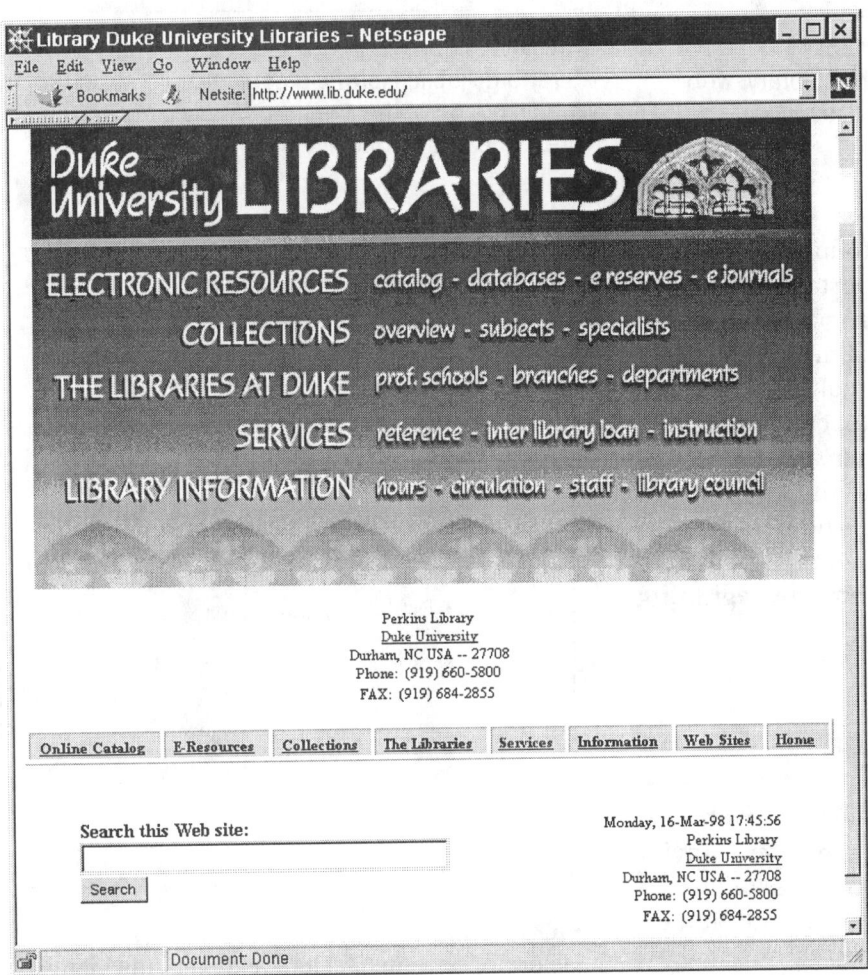

FIGURE 4.23
Duke University Libraries, table of contents and search form on the first page of the site; http://www.lib.duke.edu/

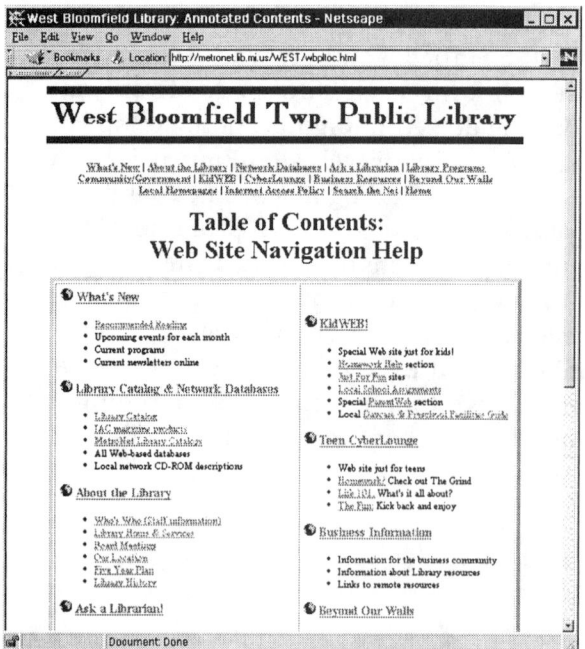

FIGURE 4.24
West Bloomfield Township Public Library, web navigation help; http://metronet.lib.mi.us/WEST/wbpltoc.html

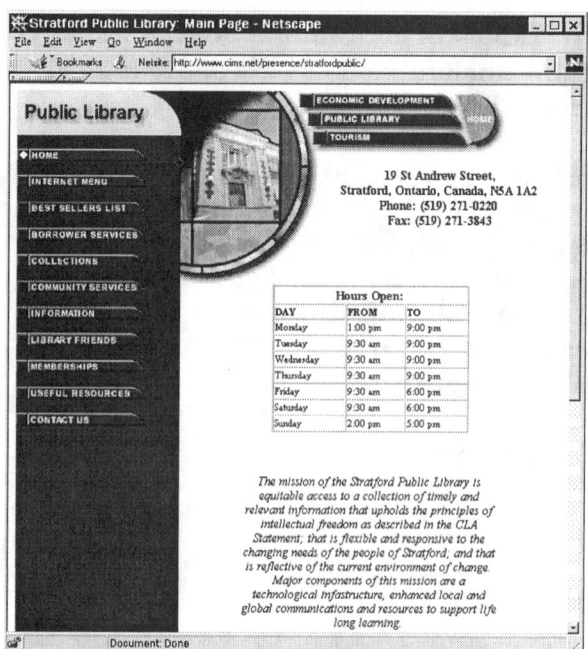

FIGURE 4.25a
Stratford Public Library, presenting site structure on the first page of the site; http://www.cims.net/presence/stratfordpublic/

Ideally, you will want to include multiple levels of navigational support in order to accommodate all users, ranging from novices to veterans. The use of multiple aids, such as a combination of toolbars, searching, and a table of contents, can be one way to achieve this goal. Another way to aid navigation is to incorporate the organization of your site into the layout and design of your first page, making the site organization and structure clear from the beginning (Figures 4.25a and 4.25b).

Consistent Navigation

To ensure that all of your library's web pages continue to provide consistent navigation, establish some guidelines for the minimal amount of information that has to be present as pages are created and updated by multiple staff members in your library. Your guidelines should refer to such conventions as:

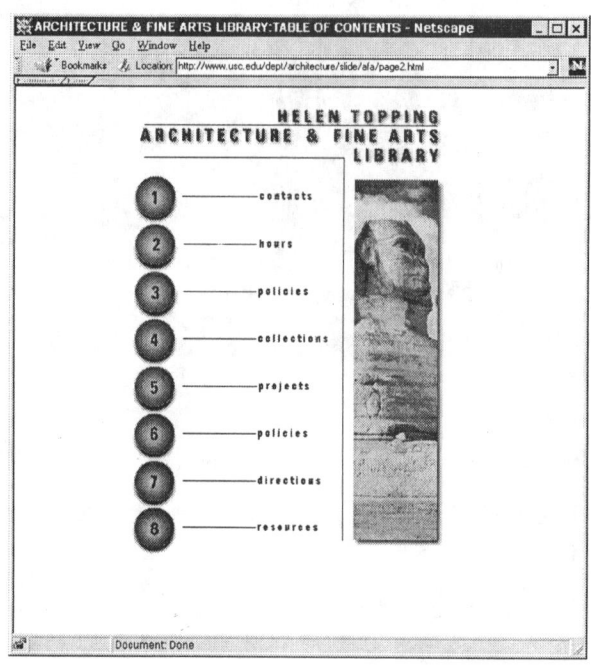

FIGURE 4.25b
Helen Topping Architecture and Fine Arts Library; incorporating site structure into page design; http://www.usc.edu/dept/architecture/slide/afa/page2.html

Including standard information in document titles. You may want to suggest that the document titles of individual pages are created in a certain form. Document titles are the titles that appear at the top of the browser window, and these are the titles that will appear in a user's bookmarks and browser history. Including the name of your library, for example, in all of your web pages will help your users remember your pages as a resource and will help alert them when they have left your pages for an external resource.

Including the name of the person creating and maintaining the page. Including the name and title of the person who created a page can give your users a sense of the reliability of the information on your library pages, and can also help personalize the site for them.

Including the e-mail address of a person or persons who can be contacted with questions or comments. Providing an e-mail address makes it possible for users to send their reactions and questions.

Keeping the date of the last revision of the web page updated. Your users need to know that the information on your web site is current and up-to-date.

These items are part of every well-designed web page and will help users anchor themselves in your site. To achieve this end, many libraries have begun creating and publishing their site-specific web guidelines for contributing staff members in order to achieve consistency throughout their sites. For example, the University of California Berkeley Library has created a document entitled *Contributing to the Library Web* and placed it on a shared server where all staff working on library web pages can access it (**http://library. berkeley.edu/Web/Markup.html**).

HTML Editors and Validators

The larger your web site becomes, and the more advanced your page design and layout get, the more confusing and tedious HTML tagging can be. Although this tagging can be done in a text editor or word processor, HTML editors can be used to make the task of modifying and creating pages less monotonous. A wide variety of HTML editors are available now, and they can be a help both to beginners and to those who are experienced in creating web pages.

HTML editors generally fall into two categories: text-based or WYSIWYG ("What You See Is What You Get"). (A list of editors by type can be found in the Appendix.) Text-based HTML editors work much like word processors but automate the process of HTML tagging. For example, you can select a phrase or section of text within your HTML text file and then select appropriate tagging from a menu. The HTML tags are then automatically inserted into place, and much typing is avoided. You can then save the file and view it in your web browser.

A WYSIWYG editor will present your file in a browser-like window. You can choose the style and placement of text and images by selecting from menu options or by highlighting and moving these elements on the page. You will see the page formatted as it will appear in a browser without seeing the HTML tagging behind it. Often in a WYSIWYG editor you can move back and forth between a browser-like window and the text background to see how the tagging has been done.

There are many functions built into HTML editors that make them a vast improvement over word processors when tagging HTML documents. Some things you might want to look for in an HTML editor are:

Spell checkers: Some editors have built-in spell checkers that will overlook HTML tags to check only the content text for errors.

Global, multifile "search and replace": This feature can make it easier to manage a site because you can update pieces of information on many or all of your files at once. For example, with this feature it would be possible to update a contact's e-mail address on many pages at once without opening and editing them individually.

Netscape and Explorer extensions: Some editors provide only standard HTML tags, while others now include the newer browser extensions. In addition, some editors let you add extensions, thereby making it possible for you to customize the editor for your personal use.

Tables: Many editors make it possible for you to insert a table into an HTML document simply by clicking on a button. You can then resize it by selecting and moving a border with your cursor. This can be much simpler than keeping track of the many layers of HTML tagging needed to create a table.

Frames: Similarly, some editors make the creation of frames much simpler by providing menu choices to produce different frame layouts and create the framed documents.

Image and color-coding functions: Color and images can often be inserted directly into an HTML file by choosing from a palette or by simply dragging an image file onto the file being edited. HTML editors also will often automatically insert the size of an image into the

tagging as the image is added, a feature which aids in quickness of loading.

Imagemap builders: HTML editors can include built-in image-mapping abilities, which make additional image-mapping software unnecessary.

These are just some of the functions available in various HTML editors. You will need to decide which particular editor has the functions that best fit your needs. Many software companies provide demonstration versions of their editors and make them available for downloading from the Web. As you prepare to choose an editor, it can be very helpful to try out these demo packages to get a sense of the one that will suit you best.

Because HTML editors can make adjusting the layout of pages much easier, experimentation with this software can go a long way in enhancing the design of your web site. While using an editor, you will often be able to try new layout designs in much less time than it would take to create the new designs using manual tagging.

One of the tricks in using HTML editors is knowing when to use a WYSIWYG editor and when to go in and edit HTML tags in a text-based HTML editor. We have found that a good strategy for creating web sites is to use a combination of editors. WYSIWYG editors, for example, are a great tool for creating the initial layout of a page because you can move elements quickly to achieve your design and see the results immediately. However, these editors often insert proprietary tagging with product identification that you will want to remove or replace with information of your own. These editors also may include tagging that does not strictly conform to standard HTML in order to achieve the layouts you create.

After the initial layout has been created in a WYSIWYG editor, it is often helpful to open the file in a text editor to make final tagging changes, or "clean up" the tagging. You may want to remove comments that have been inserted automatically by the editor. You may also want to adjust the tags that have been inserted and check them for conformity to HTML standards.

A very good way to check the correctness of the tagging in your pages after you have used an editor is to use an HTML validator, or checker. One of the most popular online tools for checking the HTML tagging in a web document is Doctor HTML (**http://imagiware.com/RxHTML**). This web site analysis program can perform a number of tests on your HTML documents and will return the results almost immediately. The tests it performs include:

- Checking the document structure for HTML tagging that might cause problems on certain browsers

- Looking at image syntax for the height, width, and ALT tags that aid in accessibility

- Examining table structure closely, as table tagging errors can occur frequently and can cause display problems in most browsers if not done correctly

Doctor HTML can also check the content within an HTML document for spelling errors and can test hyperlinks to make sure they work.

As you plan the layout of your page, keep in mind that it should always be informed by the content you are including. Experiment with tables and frames to see if they can be used to effectively present your content, being careful to incorporate appropriate navigational aids for your users. Work with editors and validators to create HTML documents that are structured carefully, as this will ensure that your web pages will display properly on the greatest number of browsers.

5 Accessible Design

In a recently released U.S. Census Bureau document, "Americans with Disabilities: 1994–95," 54 million people in the United States report having some sort of disability. Half of this population reports the occurrence of a severe disability. The definition of a disability includes "difficulty with one or more instrumental activities of daily living," or by having "one or more specified conditions." Examples included difficulty seeing, hearing, managing money, and using the telephone. The report makes it clear that what may seem to be simple activities to many can be challenges for others.

As personal computers become fixtures in homes and the popularity of the World Wide Web increases, many "activities of daily living" are now carried out online. Essential services and resources that have previously been available only through traditional means of access or carried out in person are now available through electronic means. Shopping, banking, filing of taxes, even schooling can now be accomplished through the Web. Some web forecasters predict that certain activities will become entirely digital in the future.

Just as we may endeavor to make the physical library building and resources available to patrons with disabilities, we should be equally concerned about making the library web site accessible. If you plan to offer library services such as a searchable library catalog and online submission of reference questions, these services should be available to all library patrons. Inclusiveness is the goal of an accessible web site.

The convenience and ease of online resources and services are a great advantage of the Web, and it offers tremendous potential for people with disabilities. However, the Web is not completely free of physical and intellectual barriers. Heavy use of graphics, browser-specific tags, and specialized features such as web forms can create difficulties for Internet users with visual disabilities and those using low-end browsers or low-speed Internet connections. Audio clips may render some information inaccessible to people with auditory disabilities. Improperly tagged HTML documents can make it impossible for screen-reading equipment to accurately convey the logical structure of the document. The good news is that these problems are easily corrected. A conscientious web designer can, with a little extra attention and effort, create an online environment that is accessible to a great number of people. This chapter will give you an overview of assistive technology, alert you to web barriers, and provide practical tips for designing accessible web sites.

Accessible Design and Assistive Technology

"Accessible design" and "universal design" are the phrases most often used to describe the creation of web pages that are accessible to the widest audience possible in a variety of technical environments. "Accessible tagging" is also sometimes used to indicate that HTML has been employed appropriately to achieve accessible design. Designing a web site in such a way as to make it "universally accessible" to people with disabilities or those using slow Internet connections is very important in that it benefits everyone, for *accessible* design incorporates the most essential elements of *good* design.

Along with a greater awareness of the needs of people with disabilities has come greater focus on the development of specialized technology that makes using the Web and other electronic resources easier. "Assistive technology" is often used to describe special hardware and software designed for this use. Many computer companies and software developers have special departments that design assistive technology products (Figures 5.1a and 5.1b).

Assistive technology is increasingly available in community libraries, schools, and assistive technology centers. Many different types of assistive technology are available for various computer platforms and can be used to access Internet resources:

- Screen reading software: scans the web page for text and speaks the text out loud

- Screen magnification software: used to enlarge text on a screen

- Mouse alternatives: special keyboards, voice recognition software, and other products that may be used to navigate when using a mouse is not possible

- Software utilities: software that can be loaded on your system that allows you to modify the behavior of keystrokes, alerts, and other system features

- Hardware and peripherals: refreshable Braille displays, touch screens, and personal data assistants

It is important to remember that in order to access web resources, this technology relies on the web developer to design pages in such a way that the site content may be understood and interpreted by the assistive devices. An excellent list with descriptions of different types of assistive technology is available on the University of Toronto Adaptive Technology Resource Centre web site at **http://www. utoronto.ca/atrc/tech/techgloss.html**.

Elements of Accessible Design

Designing a web site involves layers of different design elements, which, when used together, create a whole. It is critical to integrate accessible elements into each step of the design process. Avoiding flashy graphics is one way to make your site more accessible, but is not enough if you truly wish to make your web site universally accessible. Accessible design is also more than just using certain HTML tags; it also involves rethinking the organization and navigational features of a site.

FIGURE 5.1a
IBM Special Needs Systems;
http://www.austin.ibm.com/sns/

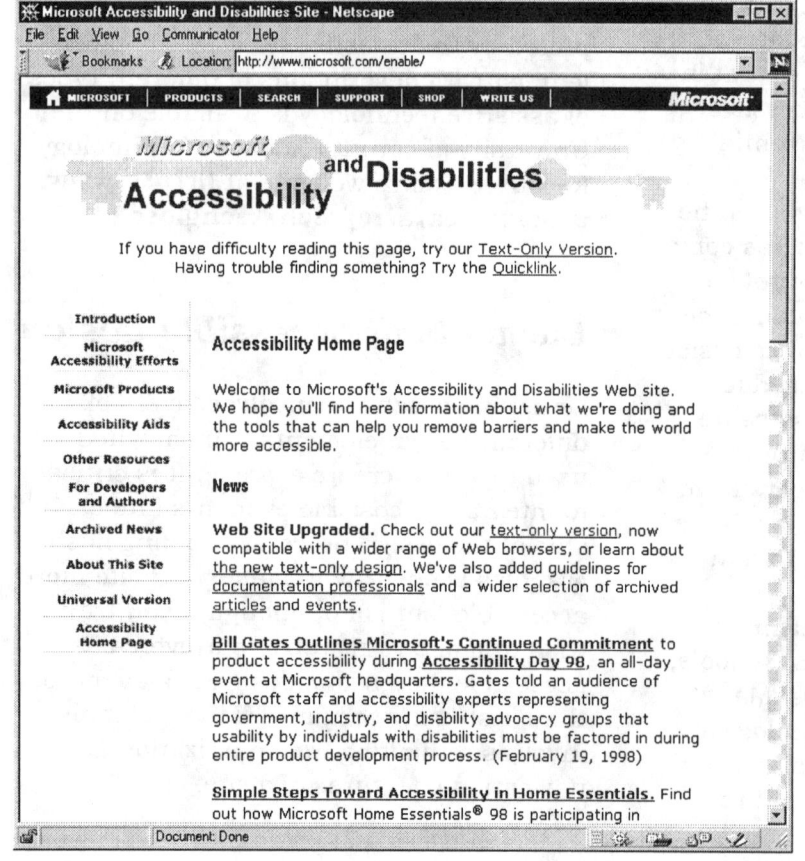

FIGURE 5.1b
Microsoft Accessibility and
Disabilities Site;
http://www.microsoft.com/enable/

Organization

The organization of a web site is perhaps the most important step in the design process. An organizational scheme should be selected based on the audience and content of the web site, and should inform all other elements of design. The information should be laid out in a logical manner, with clear header information and distinctive sections. The organization of the web pages should be kept as simple as possible, without using complicated underlying structures. Consistency in the formatting of related web pages is very important.

PRACTICAL TIPS:

Consider offering a site map and/or table of contents. A site map may be rendered as an image and allows users to see at a glance how your site is organized. A table of contents is a text alternative to a site map, which lists the main areas and sub areas of your site. Both site maps and tables of contents should be kept brief and fairly simple. They are meant to be guides, rather than exhaustive catalogs of the contents of your site (Figure 5.2).

Use logical HTML tagging. Use an <H1> for your main header, <H2> for the next subhead, and so on in sequence. Do not skip headings. Web screen-reading software looks for the headings and can read them to give the user an idea of the content of the page before reading the main text. Skipping headings or using them out of sequence will confuse the software and will not allow it to give an accurate overview of the document.

Put the most important links and information at the top of the page. People with visual disabilities cannot see formatting that may be meant to call attention to important links and information. If these items are at the top of the page they will be noticed immediately by the screen reading software.

Navigation

The next layer of design is navigation, which is closely tied to the organization of your site. Making navigational choices requires that you decide how your patrons will move through your web site. Your navigational options should be defined by the structure of your site. You will most likely want to offer an option to return to the main page of your site, options to jump to other sections of your site, perhaps an option to search the site, and a help option. You may want to make the options content-sensitive to correspond with the immediate content.

In addition to carefully selecting the navigational options to be offered, it is also important to consider how the options will be displayed. The location of the navigational options should remain consistent, perhaps always at the side or the bottom of the document. If the individual options change, certain options, such as links to the main page and to help, should always be located in the same place.

PRACTICAL TIPS:

Use carefully designed toolbars. A popular navigational device is the toolbar, which can be found on many web sites. Perhaps the most prevalent version of a toolbar is the graphical one, a narrow strip with navigational selections. A graphical toolbar may be attractive, but the selections included on it are inaccessible to a screen reader. The same problem is true for navigational buttons, another popular navigation choice. The text on a button cannot be read by a screen reader. In order to make these navigational choices available to someone using a screen reader,

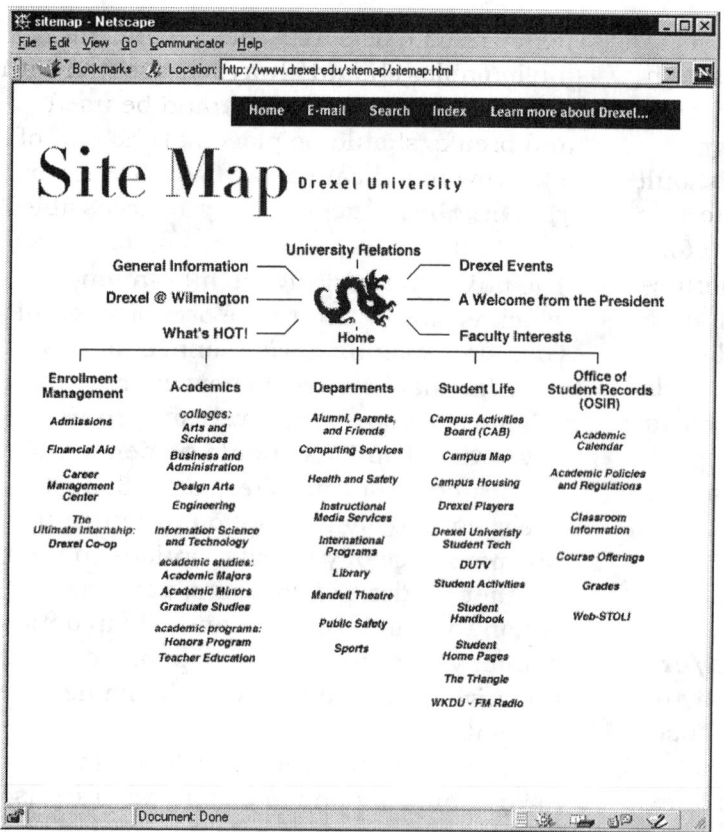

FIGURE 5.2
Drexel University—Site Map/
WGBH Boston—Table of Contents;
http://www.drexel.edu/sitemap/sitemap.
html, http://www.wgbh.org/wgbh/
sitemap.html

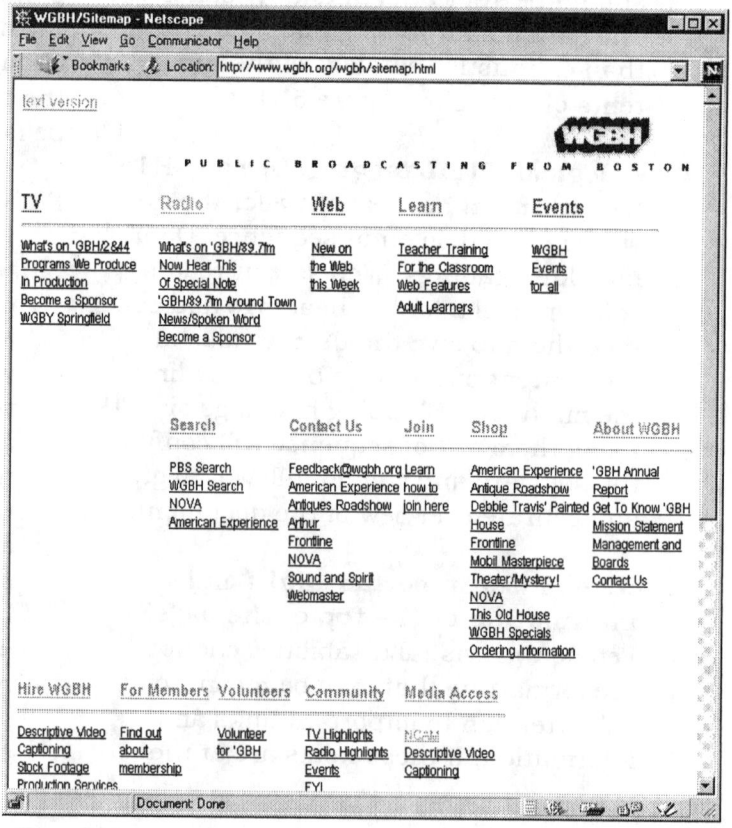

you must include ALT text for these elements, or mirror the selections with a text-based toolbar.

Do not duplicate browser options. In most cases, it is a good idea not to include options that are also offered as browser choices, such as "Back" and "Forward." These choices take up valuable space and are redundant.

Use meaningful words and phrases as links. Avoid using "click here" and other similar phrases as hyperlinks. Screen readers can be set to move from link to link in order to highlight the navigational choices. Phrases like "click here" will be meaningless. Also, graphics-only links will not be accessible and should always be accompanied by a brief text link to the same document.

Accessible Tagging

Although it is important to streamline the design of your pages to make them universally accessible, it is not necessary to completely avoid more advanced web site features. Most HTML elements can be presented so that they become accessible to all users. However, it is a good rule of thumb not to use these features indiscriminately. Frames, tables, and forms should be integrated into your web documents only when they will enhance their structure and content.

Tables

Tables are not currently handled well by screen readers, which read the screen content from left to right, line by line. Future versions of software may include better recognition of tables. If you decide to include tables on your site, use them only when necessary and provide an alternative

text version of the data included in the table. Tables should always be created with proper tagging. Headers should be used and breaks should be placed at the end of each row to indicate a new line. If you want to make your pages universally accessible, you should generally avoid using tables as a layout tool. For example, do not use tables to place text in columns. If one table is used to keep the body of the document to a certain width, it may work. However, this will slow the loading of the page and you should always check your page to ensure that the text may be read properly with screen-reading software. Lynx works well for this purpose.

Forms

Forms may be the most difficult element to deal with in terms of accessibility. However, there are some things you can do to render a form more accessible. The best approach is to offer a telephone number or e-mail address which may be used to submit the form information, or a printable version of the form with a fax number for submitting the information. Placing each form option on its own line will make it easier to navigate and distinguish between different form items.

Frames

Frames can be made accessible to most users. However, as a general design principle, frames should be used sparingly and in a minimal fashion. To make frames accessible, it is important to always include a "noframes" option. This option allows an alternative version of the page to appear when frames cannot be or are not activated. Each frame should be assigned a descriptive title which allows it to be recognized as a distinct section. Include information about the purpose of each frame.

Evaluating Your Site for Accessibility

Once you have created your pages, it is important that you check them for their level of accessibility. If you have assistive technology equipment available to you, a good approach is to test your pages using these tools. Viewing the pages on the same equipment your patrons use can give you insight into the design of your site, as well as highlight any areas that are still inaccessible or need further development. If you do not have assistive technology software and equipment in your library, you may be able to find it in other places in your community. The Alliance for Technology Access includes a list of ATA Resource Centers around the country on its web site at **http://www.ataccess.org/atacenters. html**. Many vendors of assistive technology provide samples of their products to the center, where they are made available for testing. Check with the center in your area about availability.

In addition to testing your pages with special equipment, or if assistive technology is not available to you, there are other ways to determine the accessibility of your site. Specific web sites exist that will allow you to test the conformance of your web site to accessibility standards. These sites allow you to submit the address of a web page or site to be checked for proper HTML and accessible tagging.

Bobby is a resource designed to check web pages for accessibility compliance. Bobby is provided by CAST (the Center for Applied Special Technology) and is available via a web site or as a local software application. You designate URLs for checking, Bobby examines the files, and a report is returned that indicates any accessibility problems with your document or site. If your site passes the Bobby examination, you may include a "Bobby Approved" icon on your page which indicates to your users that your site is universally accessible (Figures 5.3 and 5.4).

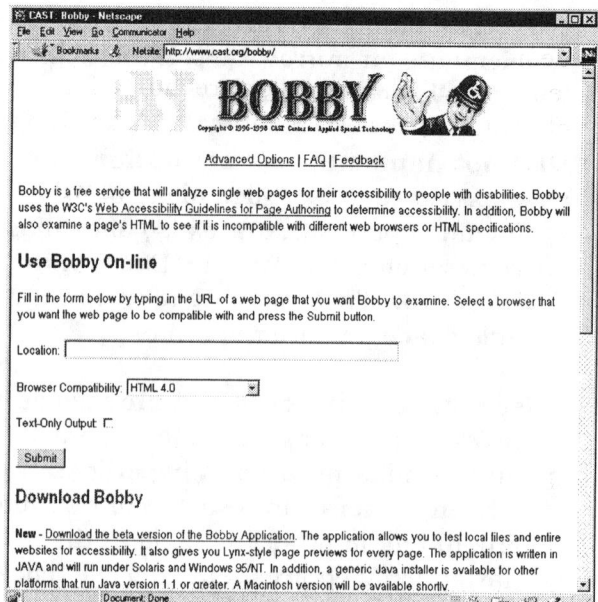

FIGURE 5.3
Bobby, a web-based validator offered by CAST; http://www.cast.org/bobby/

FIGURE 5.4
University of Illinois at Urbana-Champaign Applied Life Studies Library with the "Bobby Approved" icon; http://www.library.uiuc.edu/alx/default.asp

Doctor HTML, while not specifically designed to check for accessibility problems, is another excellent resource for checking proper HTML tagging. Like Bobby, Doctor HTML has a web interface. You enter the URL of the document you wish to check and select the preferred tests and report format. A detailed report listing and describing problems is returned within seconds (Figure 5.5).

Still one of the best tools around, Lynx can also be used to check tagging and accessibility. A nongraphical browser available on most UNIX systems, Lynx holds web pages to very strict standards. Aside from using assistive technology, Lynx may be the best tool to use to get a feel for how functional your site is for someone with a low-end computer/connection or someone with disabilities who is using screen-reader software (Figure 5.6).

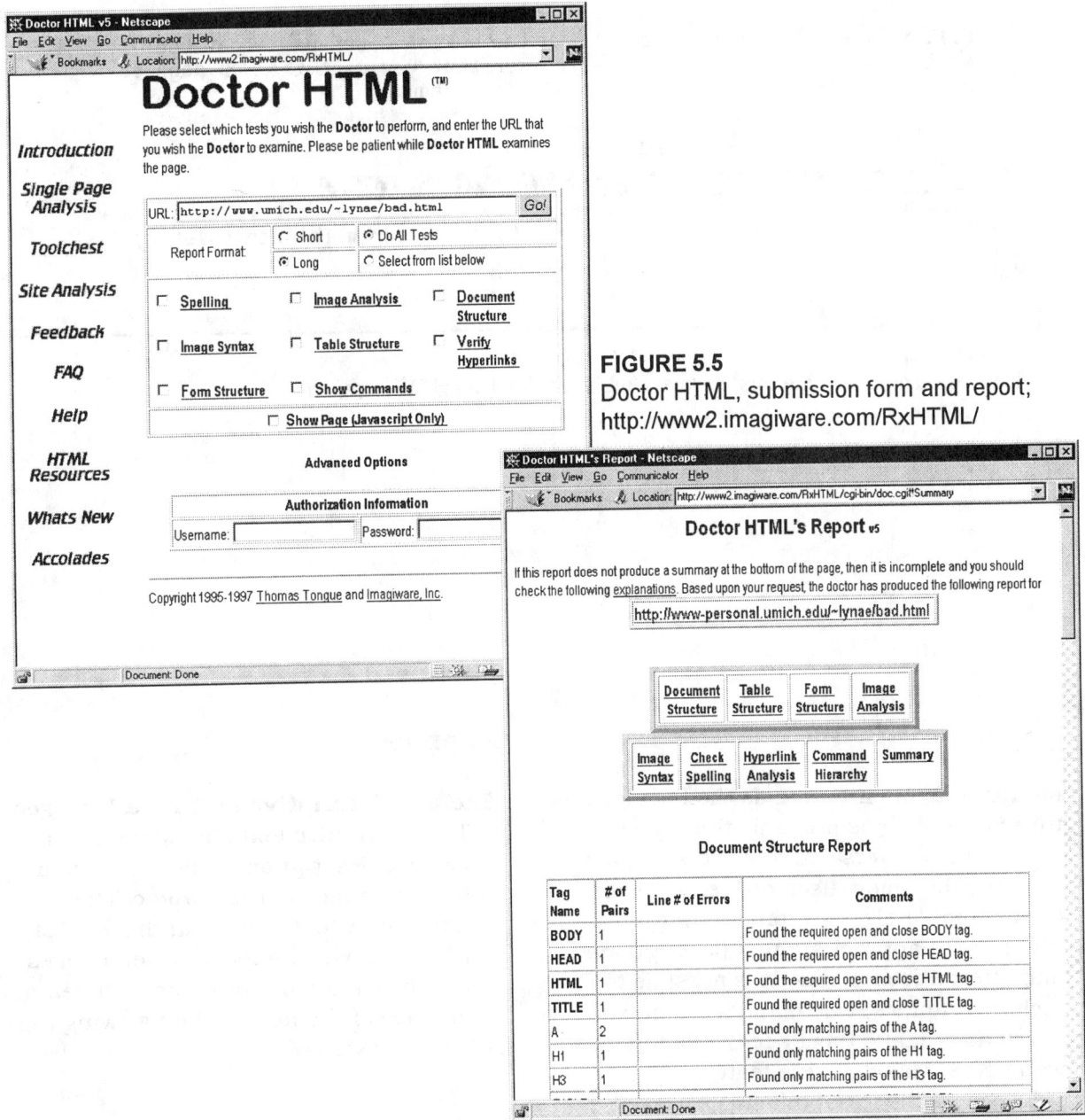

FIGURE 5.5
Doctor HTML, submission form and report;
http://www2.imagiware.com/RxHTML/

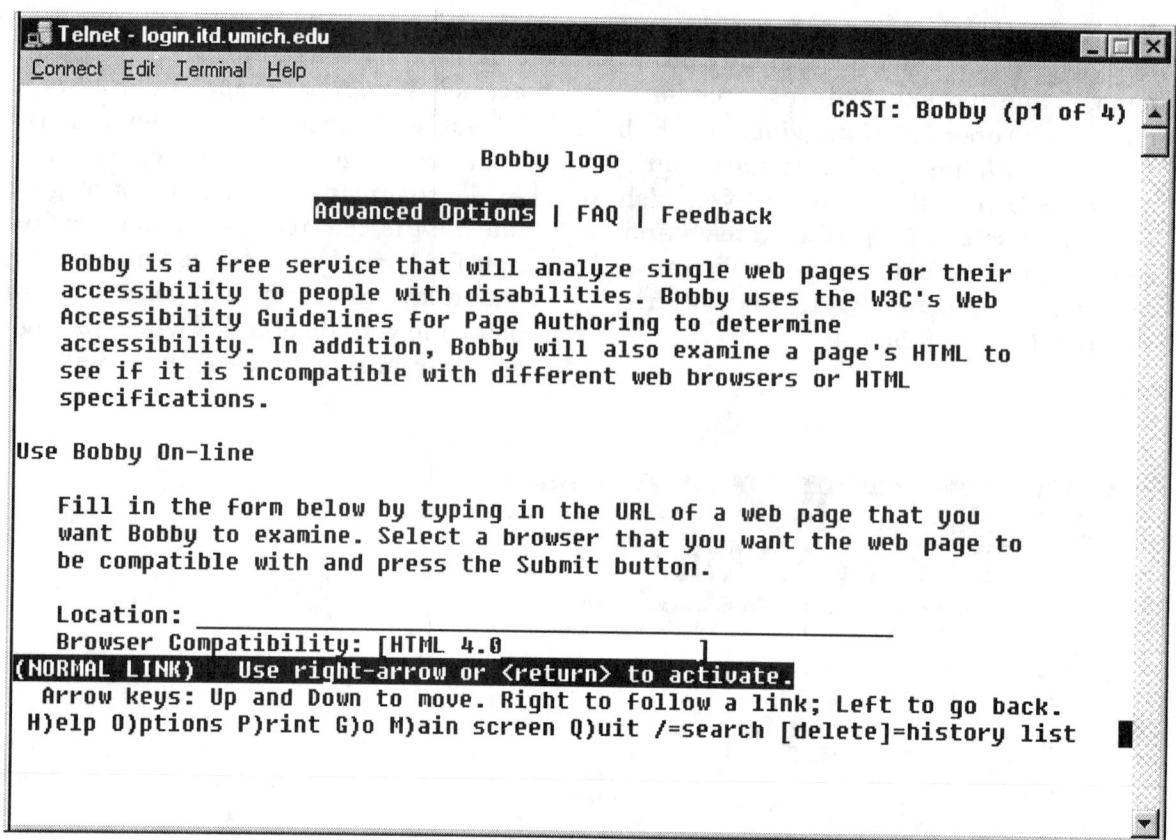

FIGURE 5.6
Lynx remains one of the best tools available for checking HTML tagging.

Use of Multimedia

Multimedia, often touted as the best feature of the Web, is probably the biggest obstacle to universal access. This is mainly because the media used on web pages is either completely gratuitous or not presented with appropriate text descriptions and alternative formats. It is possible to include graphics, video, and audio in such a way as to make them accessible to most web users. Making these features universally accessible is not difficult.

Graphics

Include descriptive text for all images.
The alternative text should include a concise description of the function and/or appearance of the graphic. The alternative text may be in the form of ALT text, which appears when images are turned off in a browser or appears in place of the image when viewing the page in Lynx.

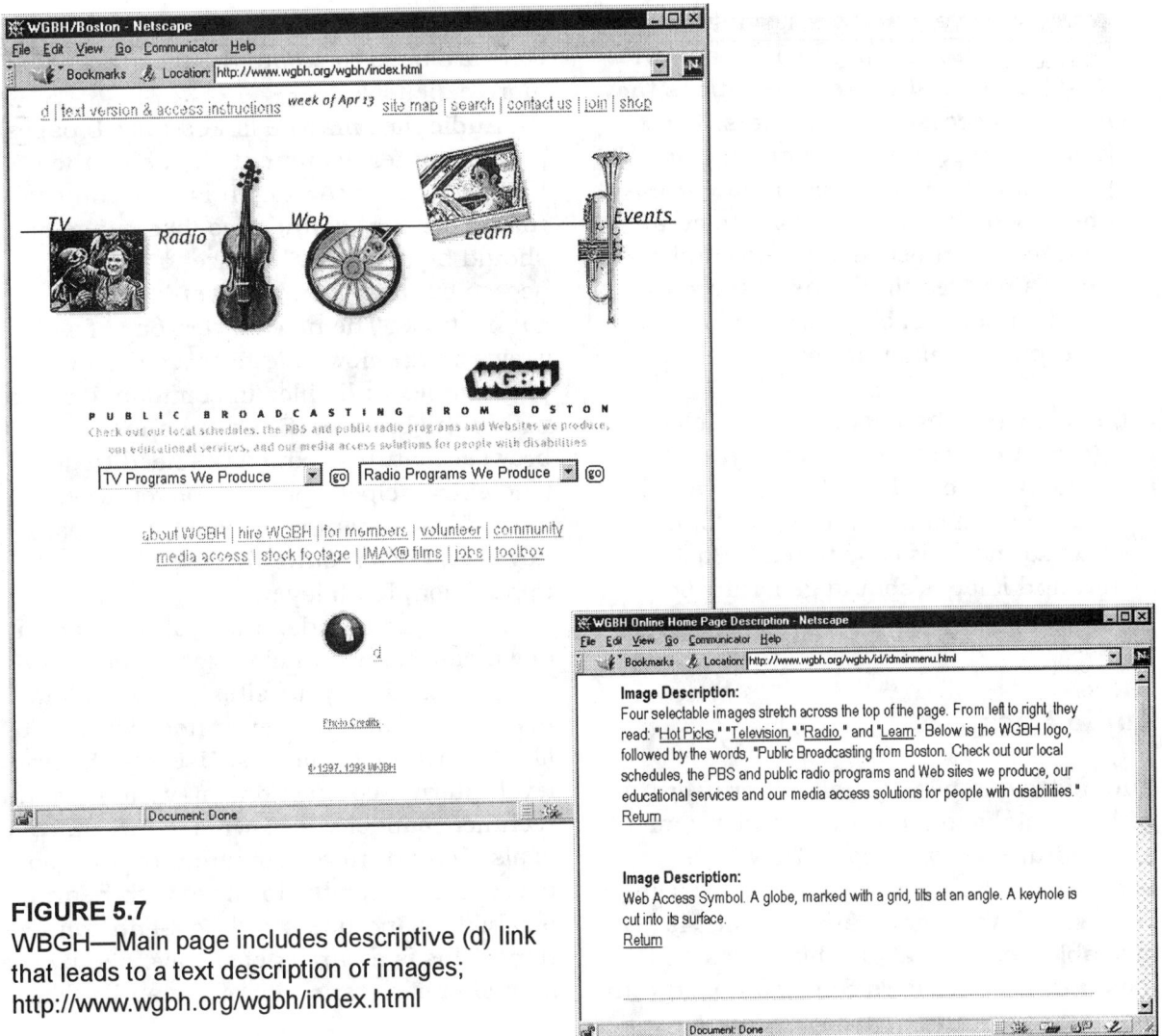

FIGURE 5.7
WBGH—Main page includes descriptive (d) link
that leads to a text description of images;
http://www.wgbh.org/wgbh/index.html

The format of an ALT tag:

> <IMG SRC="logo.gif"
> ALT="Company Logo, blue crest
> on white background">

Some designers of accessible web
sites include a "D" as a link to a
more descriptive summary next to
an image (Figure 5.7).

Use client-side imagemaps. Many
imagemaps in use on the Web are
server-side imagemaps, which require
the use of a program stored on a server.
This type of imagemap can be difficult
to create and maintain, and does not
provide an option to include ALT text for
the links included, so the navigational
options are lost unless duplicated as
text options on the page. Client-side

imagemaps are a better format for several reasons. They include an ALT text option that makes the options they contain accessible to all users. The imagemap coordinates and tagging information are included in one document, which makes it easier to create and maintain because no external program is required. The web browser on the user's machine knows how to interpret the information.

Be selective about color and background choices for your pages. Colored backgrounds should always provide enough contrast to the color of the text so that it is easy to read. Background images should generally be avoided.

Audio Files

Audio files can be very helpful for users with visual disabilities and are now common features on web sites. They have become simpler to generate and easier to access. Software for creating sounds is available free or at affordable prices and most newer computers come equipped with microphones and software needed to record sound.

Sound may be recorded and saved in several different types of audio formats, such as AIFF (Mac), WAV (PC), and AU (UNIX). It is a good idea to save your audio files in multiple formats to make it easier for patrons using different types of computers to access them. Another very popular audio format is *streamed audio*. Unlike regular audio files, streamed audio files do not need to be completely downloaded before the file begins to play, but begin playing directly after the link to the sound file is selected. The most common type of streamed audio is the RealAudio format. Streamed files are a good choice for long files and can be very accessible to people using modems. However, creating streamed

audio files is more complicated and the software used to create the files can be more expensive.

Audio files may be linked to web pages just like other documents by using the <A HREF="...">...</A> tag. It is important to remember that sound files, like image files, should be kept small in size to facilitate access by those using slower Internet connections. The newest versions of web browsers are now able to recognize and play simple audio files in common formats within the browser. Such enhanced browser features reduce the need to download extra helper applications for accessing audio files. Listening to RealAudio files, however, does require the use of a helper application, RealPlayer.

It is recommended that you include the download times and file sizes for any audio files included on your site. This will allow users to decide whether or not they would like to download the files. Users with low-level Internet connections may not have the technical capacity to download large files. It is also important to remember that audio files are inaccessible to those with hearing disabilities and users with low-end connections. This is a barrier easily avoided by the inclusion of a transcript of the audio files.

Video Captioning

Video clips are also becoming popular additions to web sites but can be inaccessible to people with visual disabilities and those using low-level Internet connections. As with audio files, descriptions and transcripts of clips that include speech should accompany videos. With readily available tools, it is now possible to produce audio descriptions and captioned videos for the Web.

The National Center for Accessible Media (NCAM), a unit of the Corporation for Public Broadcasting from Boston (CPB/WGBH), is pioneering developments in descriptive video and video captioning for the Web. NCAM is "a research and development facility that works to make media accessible to underserved populations such as disabled persons, minority-language users, and people with low literacy skills" (**http://www.wgbh.org/wgbh/pages/ncam/aboutncam.html**) (Figure 5.8). The NCAM site includes detailed directions for creating both audio descriptions of files and captioned videos for the Web. By using software and plug-ins that may be downloaded from the NCAM page, along with regular text editors, you can make video clips accessible to your users. Several examples of captioned and described videos are available on the NCAM site.

Descriptive video is video that contains an extra audio track that describes the visual elements or action taking place in the video. The descriptive track plays along with the regular audio track. If the video already contains speech, the descriptive audio track plays during pauses in the dialogue. Readily available software and a common Macintosh computer can be used to create descriptive audio tracks. The descriptive additions are recorded and inserted into the existing audio track. The use of descriptive additions and an accompanying transcript or text description can help in rendering video clips accessible to every user.

Captions may also be added to video clips using similar software. The caption text is created using a commonly available text editor and then is broken into briefer captions. The time codes for the video segment that correspond to the caption are entered into the text file. The text file is then imported into the software and saved as the text track. The videos may be viewed within certain versions of browsers or may be accessed with the use of helper applications. Some helper applications will allow the text track to be "turned off" if it is not needed for viewing.

In addition to the NCAM approach, Microsoft is developing new technology for closed captioning of video and audio files called Synchronized Accessible Media

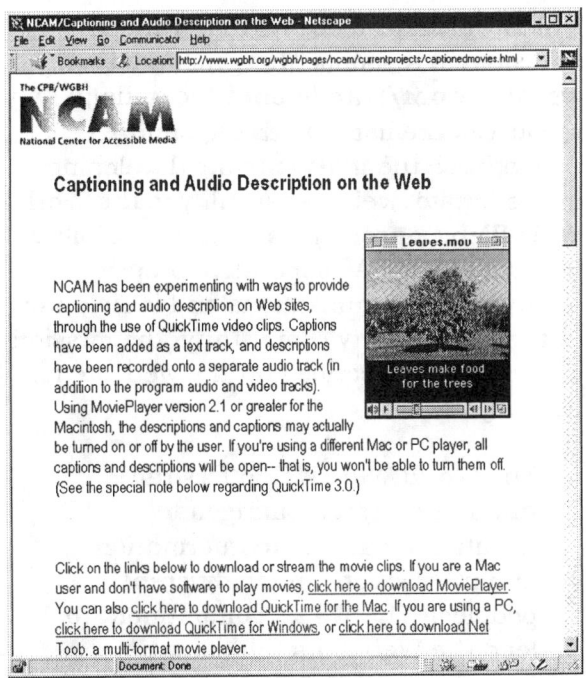

FIGURE 5.8
NCAM—Captioning and Audio Description on the Web; http://www.wgbh.org/wgbh/pages/ncam/currentprojects/captionedmovies.html

Interchange (SAMI) (**http://www.microsoft.com/enable/products/multimedia.htm**). SAMI is expected to make it easier to create captioned multimedia files and give the user more control over the presentation of the captions.

Future Developments

Awareness of the need for accessible web documents is growing. More and more web designers are getting involved, and there are many resources available for people interested in universal design. A database of accessibility resources is available on the WebABLE! site at **http://www.webable.com/webable/search.html**. The directory is provided by the Yuri Rubinsky Insight Foundation, "whose mission is to stimulate research and development of technologies which will ensure access to advanced information systems" (**http://www. webable.com/**). Additional accessibility resources are listed in the Appendix.

Perhaps the most exciting development in the area of web accessibility is the World Wide Web Consortium's Web Accessibility Initiative (WAI). A cooperative project among many organizations and individuals in the accessibility community, the mission of the WAI is described on the web site for the project:

> The World Wide Web offers the promise of transforming many traditional barriers to information and interaction among different peoples. The W3C's commitment to lead the Web to its full potential includes promoting a high degree of usability for people with disabilities. The Web Accessibility Initiative (WAI), in coordination with other organizations, is pursuing accessibility of the Web through five primary areas of work: technology, guidelines, tools, education & outreach, and research & development. (**http://www.w3.org/WAI**)

In February 1998, the first working draft of the *WAI Accessibility Guidelines: Page Authoring* was made available at **http://www.w3.org/TR/1998/WD-WAI-PAGEAUTH-0203.** (At the time of this writing, the guidelines are in the second draft stage.) The guidelines will offer general tips for accessible web design, along with accessibility criteria for specific HTML features, such as tables, forms, and frames.

Along with increased availability of resources to support the development of accessible web sites, developers of advanced web technologies are also integrating accessible features into their products.

- Microsoft, Sun Microsystems, and several other groups are working on initiatives to add accessibility features to Java.

- Developers of web editors such as HoTMetaL Pro and HomeSite are including built-in accessibility features to their products.

- Adobe maintains a server (**http:// access.adobe.com**) which will convert PDF documents to HTML or ASCII documents on-the-fly, which can then be read by screen readers.

- Many resources recommend the use of "cascading style sheets" (CSS), which allow you to define a style for multiple HTML documents by creating a type of template. This includes defining heading information, font sizes, colors, even the positioning of certain objects, such as toolbars and headers. Using CSS allows the web designer to separate the content of the web documents from the layout of the material and maintain the document structure without misusing features such as tables. As the W3C notes: "Using style sheets rather than HTML tag extensions allows the same document to be read with visual, aural, or mulitmodal presentation without cluttering up the document or having to produce three (or more) separate parallel documents which has been shown to result in update problems. This approach provides greatly improved document accessibility for visually disabled people without requiring compromises in the visual design of the document." (**http://www.w3.org/TR/NOTE-ACSS**).

Using accessible design does not consign a web designer to using only simple HTML; the key to accessible design lies in using multiple approaches. Fun and flashy HTML tags and special features do not need to be avoided altogether. You can combine them with accessible tagging and make your resources available to everyone.

6 Incorporating User Feedback into Design

It can be very easy for designers to let themselves become isolated during the design process. With a web site, like any other creation, the designer has a personal investment in the concepts, design preferences, and other elements of the site. This amount of investment in a project can sometimes result in a designer-centered approach that does not adequately incorporate feedback from others. Designing in a vacuum can lead to costly and time-consuming mistakes.

Increasingly, designers in all areas of technology are searching for ways to gather and incorporate user feedback into the process of creating a product. Who knows better the needs and preferences of an intended audience than the user himself? This thinking has led to the emerging practice of involving the intended audience in the design process, a practice which is often described as "user-centered design" (Figure 6.1). In addition to avoiding potentially costly and time-consuming mistakes, there are many other reasons why incorporating user feedback into the design process is a good idea.

FIGURE 6.1
Web Review: Usability Matters Design Studio, promoting "user-centered design"; http://webreview.com/97/04/25/usability/index.html

It keeps you in touch with your audience. Designers who avoid soliciting user feedback may find that they only hear from their users when there is a problem. Communicating with users only when they report errors may put the designer in a reactive, even defensive position which isolates the designer from the users. Being proactive in consulting users before, during, and after the design process creates a much more positive design environment, and will help you stay in touch with your audience's needs and preferences.

It keeps you up-to-date with new developments. A proactive and inclusive design approach will also help you remain up-to-date with new web developments. Collaboration, collegial activity, and communication with dedicated users can be great ways of continuing education.

Audiences contribute valuable ideas. While you will do your best as a web designer to anticipate the information needs of your users, you will not be able to think of everything. Often the best ideas can come from your users, who have a different perspective on the resource. The user is sometimes in a better position to be objective, and may be aware of resources and developments you are not aware of (Figure 6.2).

It creates "buy-in" on the part of the users. Involving users in the design process gives them a voice. Having a voice and contributing to the process imparts the same feeling of personal investment that the web designer experiences. The investment creates "buy-in" on the part of audience, which helps ensure continued support for the project.

It generates publicity. Involving the intended audience in the design of the site, and keeping them updated about

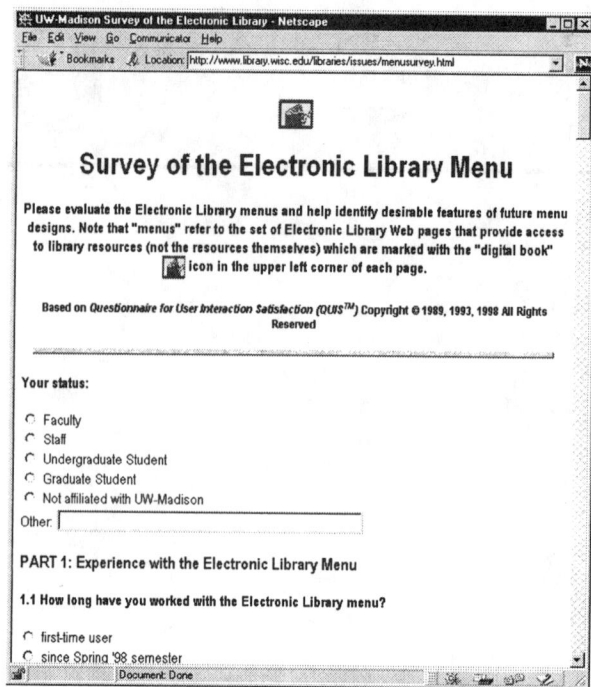

FIGURE 6.2
University of Wisconsin-Madison Libraries–Survey of the Electronic Library Menu, gathering user feedback for web page evaluation; http://www.library.wisc.edu/libraries/issues/menusurvey.html

progress, can generate publicity for the site by encouraging regular communication and stimulating interest in new developments. The evolution of a web site keeps the resource interesting and dynamic.

Iterative Design

Involving users in the design of your site should be a regular part of its maintenance and updating processes. The most extensive user evaluation and review may take place at the beginning of the process, as you gather ideas and develop a prototype. This is typically considered the most important time for consulting your audience to confirm your choices and design. However, user input will be valuable throughout the life of your project. Many resources that have disappeared from the web horizon were those that failed to evolve with the needs and interests of the users.

Iterative design is an approach to web development that you may want to consider. In the iterative design process, a project prototype is created, tested, redesigned, released, and re-evaluated periodically. This approach to designing web resources offers many advantages over long development times that are spent trying to create the perfect web site. With the iterative approach, a site prototype can be created, viewed, and evaluated by a small subset of users who identify problems and suggest changes. Once the immediate problems are corrected and suggestions are implemented, the site is released to the larger audience, who become part of the design and quality control team by using and evaluating the resource and sharing their feedback with the developers. The developers fix problems and integrate user suggestions into the resources, and the cycle continues.

This approach may be especially useful to web designers because of the ever-changing nature of the Internet and web resources. Think back to the early days of the Internet when gophers offering hierarchical text files were the exciting Internet development. In an incredibly short time, gophers were replaced by multitudes of complex web sites that offer elaborate multimedia experiences and important services. In order to keep up with the fast pace of Internet development, you must plan for periodic updating of your site. Iterative design can be a useful tool for keeping your resource up-to-date with new web developments.

Gathering User Feedback

There are many different mechanisms for gathering feedback from your users and initiating user evaluation. Providing contact information, feedback forms, and directed evaluations are the most prevalent options. These different mechanisms require different amounts of time and effort to plan, implement, and maintain.

In order to select the best method for gathering user feedback, you need to know your resource. It is critical that you remain familiar with the content of your site and always keep in mind its goals and audience. You must also stay in touch with web developments. New options for interactive web sites are continually becoming available, and new information about user evaluation methods is constantly being shared within the web design community.

It is also very important that you keep records of your ideas, changes, and previous versions of documents as you develop your site and make changes to it. These records will allow you to track the development of a web page. This record keeping also ensures that if you decide not to implement a suggestion immediately, you will have a record of it for future development of your resource. No one is perfect and technical problems do happen. It is possible that a change may not work out, or you may lose files. Storing previous versions of your documents will allow you to return to or reconstruct a former version.

You will need to remember that each type of feedback mechanism will require a different amount of effort on the part of both the designer and the user. The different types of feedback mechanisms will result in different types and amounts of feedback. For these reasons, it can be a good idea to use multiple options at different stages of the design process.

Mailto Links

A "mailto" address is a special HTML tag that may be included in your web documents. Selecting a mailto link will trigger an e-mail program and present the user with a blank e-mail message addressed to the address included in the tag. The mailto tag looks like this:

> Send your feedback to <A HREF="mailto:jane.doe@domain.com"> jane.doe@domain.com</A>.

The user will see it this way:

> Send your feedback to jane.doe@domain.com.

Clicking on the link will automatically open up an e-mail program. The user will then be able to send a message to the e-mail address specified.

Using the mailto tag is one mechanism that may be used to solicit feedback, and is probably the easiest to implement. However, it is also the least structured option. If you expect feedback through a mailto link, you must encourage the use of this feature by your users. The mailto tag is probably best used as a general communication tool. It may be helpful to think of it as the equivalent of offering a phone number—you must still rely upon the user to choose to submit a question or comment.

Web Forms

Web forms are another HTML-based tool that may be used to gather feedback (Figure 6.3). Web forms may be used to solicit more structured feedback than is possible with a mailto link. However, it is true that the more structure a tool offers, the more effort it requires on the part of the web designer.

Web forms offer a variety of features which allow the designer to guide the user's comments, but also allow the user to enter free-form questions. Some of these features are:

- text entry fields

- pop-up menus

- check boxes

While the HTML tags used in web forms are easy to learn and manipulate, these forms do require a special program in order to deliver the contents to their destination. This software must be available on the server you are using. It collects the data submitted through the form and sends it to a predetermined location, usually an e-mail address or special database. If you are not familiar with such software, you may want to consult a system administrator when planning a web form.

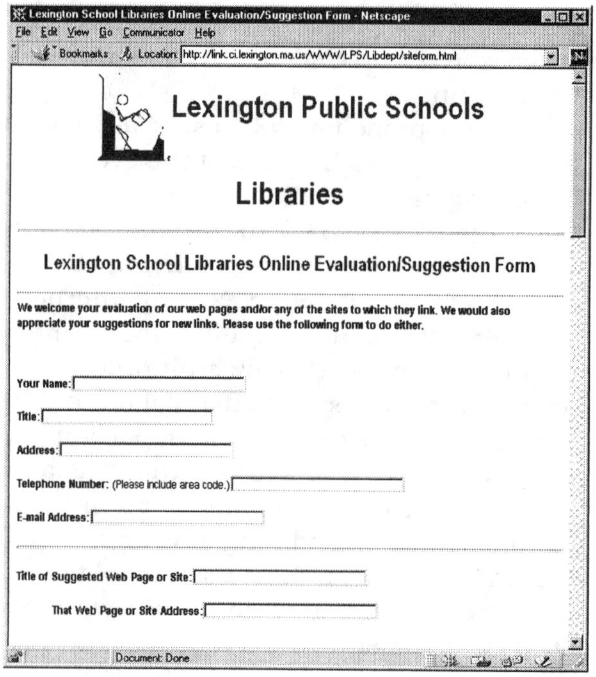

FIGURE 6.3
Lexington Public School Libraries—Online Evaluation/Suggestion Form, using an HTML form to gather feedback; http://link.ci.lexington.ma.us/WWW/LPS/Libdept/siteform.html

Surveys

Surveys are a more traditional method of gathering user feedback. A survey may be conducted in the form of a telephone call, a printed document, or a web form. Surveys usually require much more time on the part of the developer for selecting questions, identifying and contacting respondents, and analyzing responses. The advantage of a survey, though, is that it may be used to solicit much more specific and directed feedback (Figure 6.4).

If you choose to use a survey, you may wish to use a web form and place it on your web site for a certain period of time. In some instances, web site developers insert the survey between a linking page and the main page of a resource. This can be a tricky situation—some users may be irritated by this approach. An alternative approach is to set the survey so that it opens in a separate window, or is a completely voluntary choice on your site. If you plan to invest time in creating a survey, you should be sure that you will receive thoughtful responses. Making the survey as painless as possible will help encourage responses.

User Evaluation

User evaluation is perhaps the most valuable type of user feedback mechanism. It is a time-intensive approach but is probably the best tool for creating user buy-in and gaining relevant feedback. User evaluation is especially important for a resource that is going to require a big investment of staff time and resources.

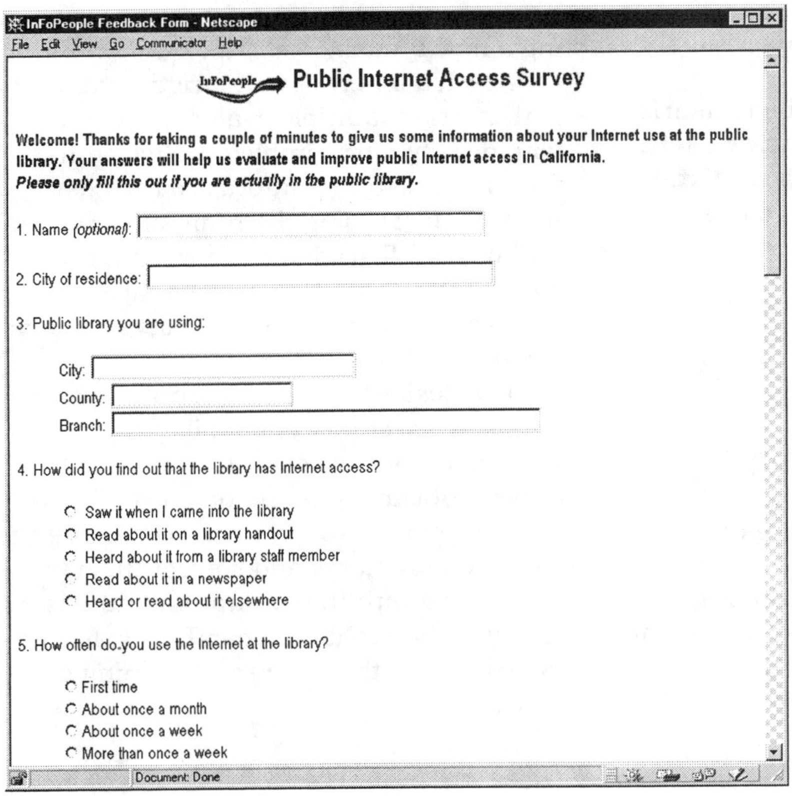

InFoPeople Feedback Form - Netscape

File Edit View Go Communicator Help

InFoPeople Public Internet Access Survey

Welcome! Thanks for taking a couple of minutes to give us some information about your Internet use at the public library. Your answers will help us evaluate and improve public Internet access in California.
Please only fill this out if you are actually in the public library.

1. Name *(optional)*:

2. City of residence:

3. Public library you are using:

City:
County:
Branch:

4. How did you find out that the library has Internet access?

- Saw it when I came into the library
- Read about it on a library handout
- Heard about it from a library staff member
- Read about it in a newspaper
- Heard or read about it elsewhere

5. How often do you use the Internet at the library?

- First time
- About once a month
- About once a week
- More than once a week

Document: Done

FIGURE 6.4
InFoPeople Project—Public Internet Access Survey, one method for soliciting feedback; http://infopeople.berkeley.edu:8000/ipeval.html

For example, in creating an online version of an existing product, think about the current advantages and disadvantages of that product. What do you want to carry through to the online version? What do you want to change? What can you do in the new environment that couldn't be achieved in the former environment? Your users may have the best answers to these questions, and user evaluation can help you detect them.

One type of user evaluation that is being adopted by more and more designers is *heuristic evaluation*. Defined by Jakob Nielsen, heuristic evaluation is

a usability engineering method for finding the usability problems in a user interface design so that they can be attended to as part of an iterative design process. Heuristic evaluation involves having a small set of evaluators examine the interface and judge its compliance with recognized usability principles (the heuristics). (**http://www.useit. com/papers/heuristic/ heuristic_evaluation.html**)

Nielsen lists ten basic usability heuristics on his web site at **http://www.useit. com/papers/heuristic/heuristic_list. html**. Nielsen's heuristics are general principles for all types of systems:

1. Visibility of system status
2. Match between system and the real world
3. User control and freedom
4. Consistency and standards
5. Error prevention
6. Recognition rather than recall
7. Flexibility and efficiency of use
8. Aesthetic and minimalist design
9. Help users recognize, diagnose, and recover from errors
10. Help and documentation

Keith Instone, working from these principles, has modified them to be applicable specifically to web resources (**http:// webreview.com/97/10/10/usability/ sidebar.html**).

Heuristic evaluation can be a very good approach for libraries. It is easy to understand and can give a beginner the basic structure for an evaluation process. Heuristic evaluation does not require great technical knowledge or an extensive background in evaluation techniques. It is cost-efficient, can be accomplished with minimal staff, and can be modified to fit your needs.

Heuristic evaluation involves enlisting the assistance of evaluators who receive heuristics compiled by the system designers. Evaluators are instructed to identify usability problems. Working alone, they navigate through and use the system, applying the heuristics to their experiences and noting usability problems. Evaluators may be asked to record their experiences, or an "observer" may record the activity. It is acceptable to provide the evaluators with a "usage scenario" to help guide them through the system. Usage scenarios may be especially important if you are developing a new system.

An idea inherent in heuristic evaluation is that using multiple evaluators can help you identify more problems. Nielsen has found that 3–5 evaluators are the best number. Increasing the number of evaluators beyond five adds more work for the coordinators and does not significantly increase the number of usability problems located.

The desired result of heuristic evaluation is an inventory of usability problems. The evaluators are expected only to identify these problems. It is the responsibility of the designers of the system to examine the identified problems and correct them. Consulting with the evaluators and observers after the evaluation can be a valuable experience in the process of defining solutions.

This approach can be easily applied to the evaluation of a web-based online catalog. The staff member coordinating the project compiles the heuristics and creates some usage scenarios. Evaluators can be interested patrons, members of a youth advisory group, library board members, etc. An observer watches the evaluators and notes usability problems. The coordinator, observer, and evaluators meet to discuss the experience and perhaps brainstorm about solutions.

Heuristic evaluation can be a very positive experience for all people involved in the process. The voices of library users are heard, the burden of testing and evaluation is distributed among more people, and potential usability problems are identified and addressed in advance of the release of the system. A complete heuristic evaluation approach may be overkill for certain resources or web sites. However, there is much to learn from heuristic evaluation and the approach can be modified to fit your needs.

Web Statistics

In addition to user evaluation, web statistics can be another helpful tool for assessing the use of your resource. Access information gathered by your server can tell you many things about the use of your resource, including the type of browser your patrons use, which features of your site are heavily/seldom used, whether or not your users encountered any technical problems, and where your users are located.

This information, pulled from the access files and run through a web statistics program, can provide some meaningful information that can be used to inform the design of your site. You can track system usage and forecast growth, which may help

you decide if or when you need to upgrade your software or server for better performance. Usage data for your site can help you identify resources with low use that need to be highlighted or removed. You may be able to determine if your patrons are accessing your site from home or within the library, and what browser and version they are using, which should influence your design choices and planning for support.

The limitations of web statistics are numerous and the data can be difficult to manage. The usage data collected are rough information in a raw format. Because users generally do not sign on with a username and password when they use a web resource, information related to user sessions is difficult to achieve. There is also the question of defining a hit or access and pulling out meaningful accesses. You must know your system and be able to isolate the relevant information and mold it into a useful format.

Making Use of Web Statistics

All web resources generate some type of a *log file*, which records every "hit" or access to a web site. The format of the log files depends somewhat on the server software you are using. The most general format of a log file is the "common log file." This type includes the most basic information: the host information for the user, the time of the access, and the path name of the document that was accessed. A more useful format of log file is the "combined log file," which includes information about type of browser used and the page followed to that URL.

The following information can be retrieved from a combined log format (Figure 6.5):

1. **123.456.78.9**

   User's IP address/domain information: the unique address of each machine connected to the Internet. This information can be used to do what is called a *reverse lookup*. The numerical IP information is matched with domain name information and may be used to determine the type of domain your users are coming from (.edu= educational, .com=commercial, .org= organization).

2. **[04/Apr/1998:00:01:15 -0500]**

   Date and time of the access.

3. **"GET /cgi-bin/test/sample.html HTTP/1.0"**

   Action taken. In this case, access to an HTML file. Indicates the specific file accessed (sample.html).

4. **"Mozilla/3.01Gold (Win95; I)"**

   Browser version being used by your user, in this case Netscape 3.01 Gold.

5. **200**

   Code that indicates a successful hit. Page was accessed without problems

6. **14209**

   Number of bytes transmitted for this request.

7. **"http://www.test.org/test/"**

   Referring URL: the URL of the page that included the link se lected to access the current page. This information can sometimes be used to follow the user's path through your database, or to see how people locate your resource through links on other web sites.

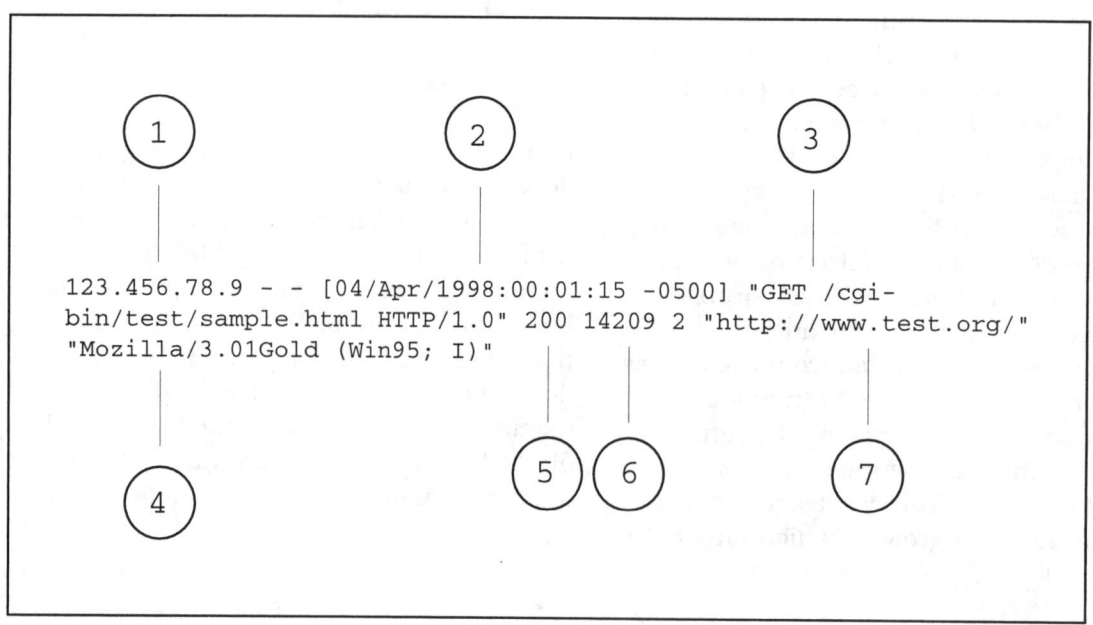

FIGURE 6.5
Sample "combined log file"

In order to obtain this type of information, you must set up your server software to store and maintain the log files, be able to access the log file contents and extract meaningful information, and you must acquire statistics software that will allow you to manipulate the log file data and define report formats. The most important, and perhaps the most difficult, part of this process is defining the meaningful information. In order to define a meaningful access for your web site, you must have extensive knowledge of your own product. You need to know the different elements of your site and what the function of each element is. Then you must select the elements that illustrate meaningful information.

If your resource is stored on a centralized server, the mechanisms for obtaining access to your log file data may already be in place. Check with your system administrator to verify this. If these mechanisms are not in place, you may need to start from scratch. Depending on your level of comfort with your server software and your technical skills, you may need to consult with or enlist the skills of a system administrator.

If you subscribe to an online commercial resource, check with the vendor about their provision of statistics. They may already provide usage information for your site. Most vendors will provide some sort of usage data, if only basic access counts. If your vendor does not provide this information, or provides little information, you may want to pursue this issue. They may be able to produce data for you or in a format that you may manipulate.

Privacy is an important issue to consider when using access data from your resource. The host information that is recorded in the access files can sometimes identify individual users. Many IP addresses are static—assigned to a specific machine. If the machine is located in a home or a private office, the person using the machine may be identified. Existing library policies may help you with this issue. The approach you take to protecting

circulation records should also be extended to electronic resources, especially if you plan to post your usage information on your web site or share it in some way.

Another consideration is the format of the statistical report. Most statistical packages will produce tabular information. You may find that charts can be helpful, though, especially when comparing data from different time periods. Some statistics packages allow you to produce graphs of your usage data.

Web counters are basic tools used to count accesses to web pages. There are many public domain and commercial counters available, from very simple counters that record the number of hits to a page to more advanced counters that distinguish between different types of accesses and produce usage reports. Counters are available as cgi scripts, java applets, and as "hosted counters"—counter services that are maintained on remote servers. *CounterGuide.Com* (**http://www.counterguide.com/**) is a great resource for information about counters and links to counter software (Figure 6.6a).

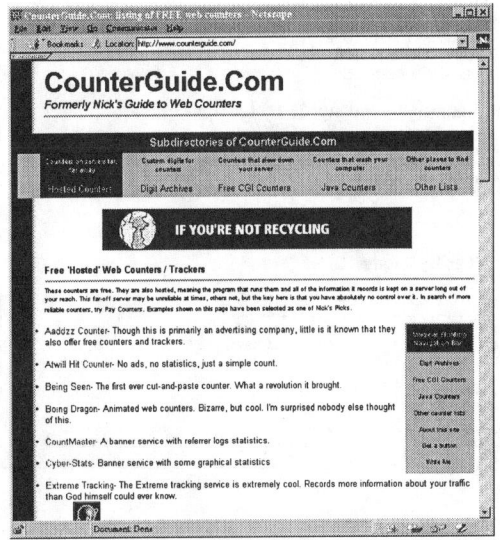

FIGURE 6.6a
The CounterGuide, a site with links to counter software; http://www.counterguide.com

Log analysis tools are the most common type of software used to analyze web site usage statistics. Log analysis tools are often designed for UNIX-based web sites (written in the perl programming language) and work by extracting specified data from the log files collected on the web server. Many log analysis tools are available as freeware and shareware. These tools analyze log files and produce reports in HTML format. Popular packages include wwwstat (**http://www.ics.uci.edu/pub/websoft/wwwstat/**) and Analog (**http://www.statslab.cam.ac.uk/~sret1/analog/**) (Figures 6.6b and 6.7). A program that works with wwwstat and produces graphs of the usage data is gwstat (**http://dis.cs.umass.edu/stats/gwstat.html**). It may be possible to modify shareware log analysis tools to fit your needs. Such modifications of the software will require programming skills.

These types of log analysis tools will probably suit the needs of most web developers. However, if you manage a large site or a heavily used resource, you may want to look into commercial software. Commercial software can be expensive ($300–$10,000+) and is generally designed with for-profit businesses in mind. Rather than using a log file analysis approach, many commercial software packages are loaded onto the web server and analyze the data in "real time," as users access the resource. Commercial software may also offer additional advantages such as well-designed report formats and technical support. A list of commercial products is available from Yahoo at **http://www.yahoo.com/Business_and_Economy/Companies/Computers/Software/Internet/World_Wide_Web/Log_Analysis_Tools/**.

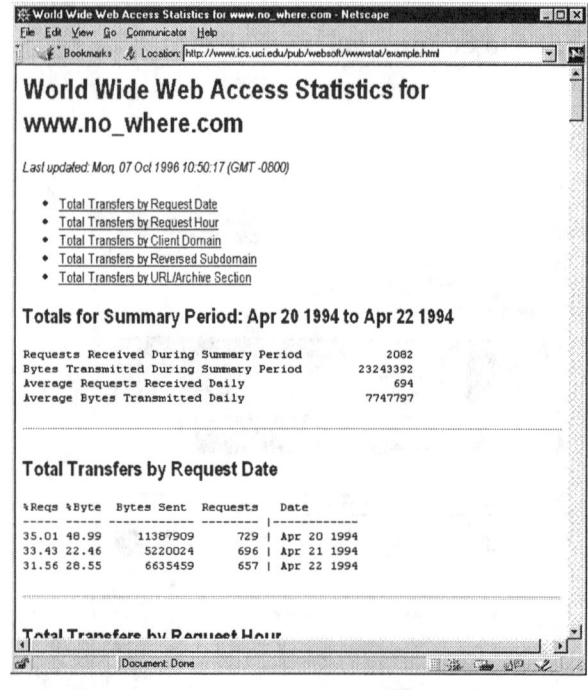
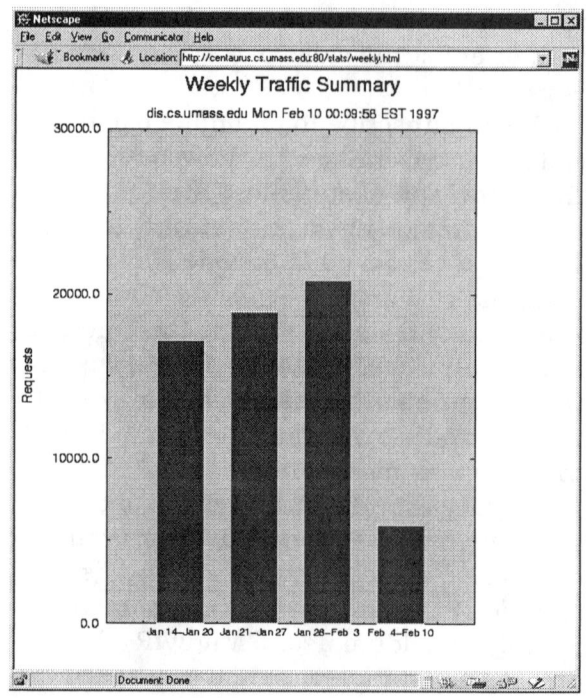

FIGURE 6.6b
Sample wwwstat and gwstat reports;
http://www.ics.uci.edu/pub/websoft/wwwstat/;
http://dis.cs.umass.edu/stats/gwstat.html

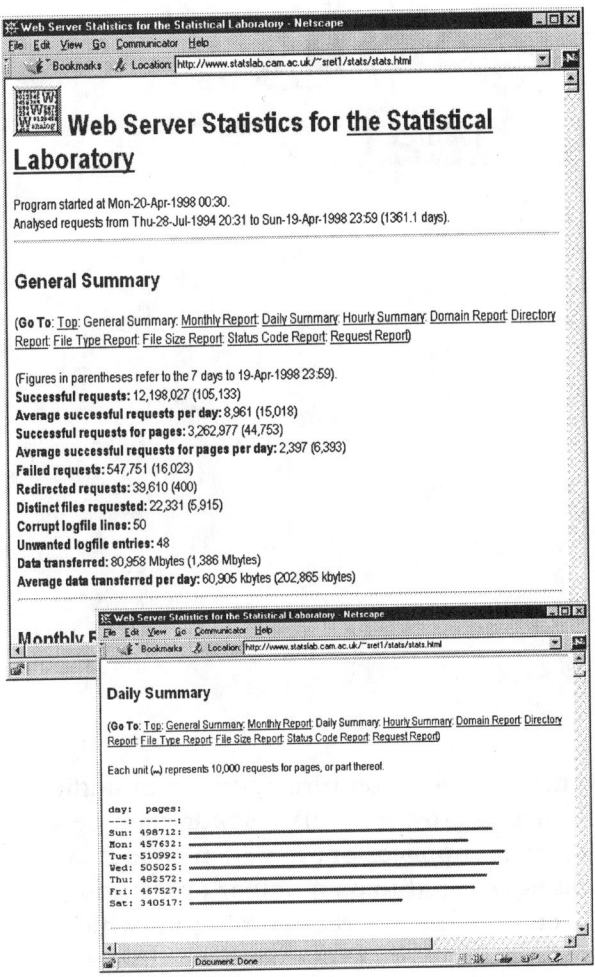

FIGURE 6.7
Analog report sample

Things to Keep in Mind

Beware of designing for individuals. As a web designer, it is very natural to want to please every member of your intended audience. When you receive comments about your resources, how-ever, it can be difficult to determine if this is a concern of one person or many. But, you should try to avoid changing things immediately upon receiving a report of a problem or a suggested change. Investigate and take the time to figure out if the "problem" is really a design flaw or is perhaps just an individual preference. If you react before evaluating the problem, you may find yourself in the precarious position of trying to please everyone.

Define your expectations for the evaluation process. Before you ask your users for feedback, you must decide what you want and need to know. Useful feedback will be easier to achieve if you give your evaluators some direction. It is necessary to decide what level of input you would like. Do you just want to confirm that your resource is getting use? Would you prefer to know which specific documents are most useful? Do you need user input at the beginning of the process in order to define your project? These are examples of the types of questions a web designer should ask before initiating any type of user evaluation.

Balance expected effort with expected return. Neglecting to include user feedback in your design plans, or only giving user feedback small consideration in your plans, can be a big mistake. You must carefully consider what type of feedback you need and how much time you will spend on it. It is probably not worthwhile to spend a lot of time and effort to get extensive feedback regarding one feature of a site or resource. You must weigh expected effort against desired return. The goal is to achieve balance.

7 Looking Ahead

Libraries are rapidly developing their web sites, which are often among the most advanced on the Web. Many libraries now have staff members that work full-time on their library's web site, and position titles such as electronic resources librarian or digital librarian are cropping up more often. It is also not uncommon to see librarians referring to themselves as "webmasters." As librarians continue this involvement with the Web, and as they continue to refine the ways in which they use it to provide their resources, they are increasingly looking ahead to emerging technologies that can be used on their web sites to further expand their levels of online service. In this chapter, we will describe a few of the most promising new technologies and some of the ways in which they are starting to be used in libraries.

New Developments

Many of the new technologies librarians are using augment standard HTML documents and, therefore, require software in addition to a web browser. This software can be an external application, in which case it is often referred to as a helper application. Or, it can be in the form of a plug-in, which is a form of software that opens within a web browser's window in order to present special file formats. Although the software used to create the external files themselves usually needs to be purchased, the necessary helper applications and plug-ins tend to be freely available for users.

Adobe Acrobat

Adobe Acrobat PDF (Portable Document Format) files are frequently used in conjunction with HTML documents on a web site. These files are very useful if you have paper-based information that you want converted to an electronic format but that still needs to be printed out exactly as it appears in the original print format. Some examples of this type of information include contracts, legal documents, newsletters, or library handouts.

Since PDF files are quite easy to create, they can be a convenient format for putting many of your library's print items on your web site. For example, if you plan to add the new issue of your library newsletter to your site each week or month, it could be much easier and faster to convert the print item to PDF than to create an HTML version (Figure 7.1). An added advantage to using a PDF file for this task is that any unique formatting or graphics will be retained in the final electronic version.

It is possible to search for words or phrases within text-based PDF files. You can also zoom in or out to focus on certain portions of text and move from page to page quickly. Libraries are finding other uses for PDF files in order to take advantage of these capabilities. For example, some libraries, in cooperation with instructors, are putting information that has been converted to PDF in their online class reserves (Figures 7.2a and 7.2b). This makes distributing and viewing the information very convenient for students and faculty. PDF files also print easily, which can be a big advantage for students, instructors, and librarians.

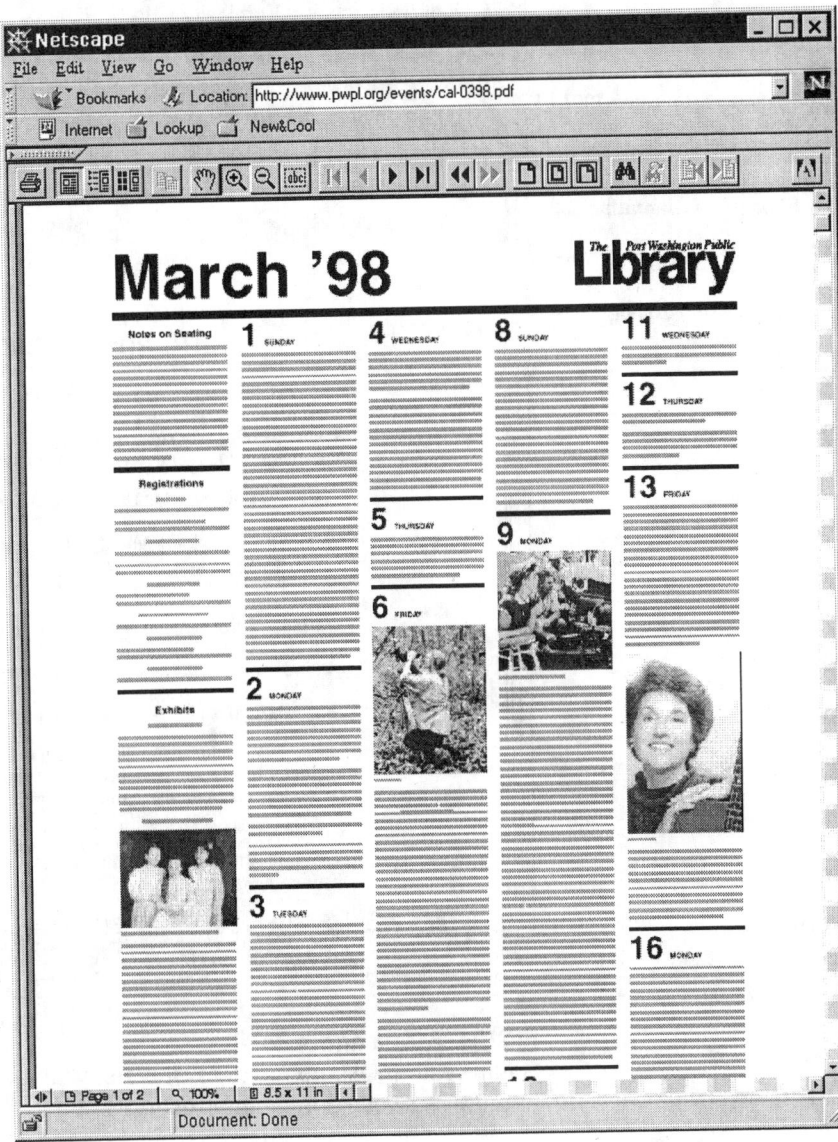

FIGURE 7.1
Port Washington Public Library, monthly newsletter in PDF; http://www.pwpl.org/events/cal-0398.pdf

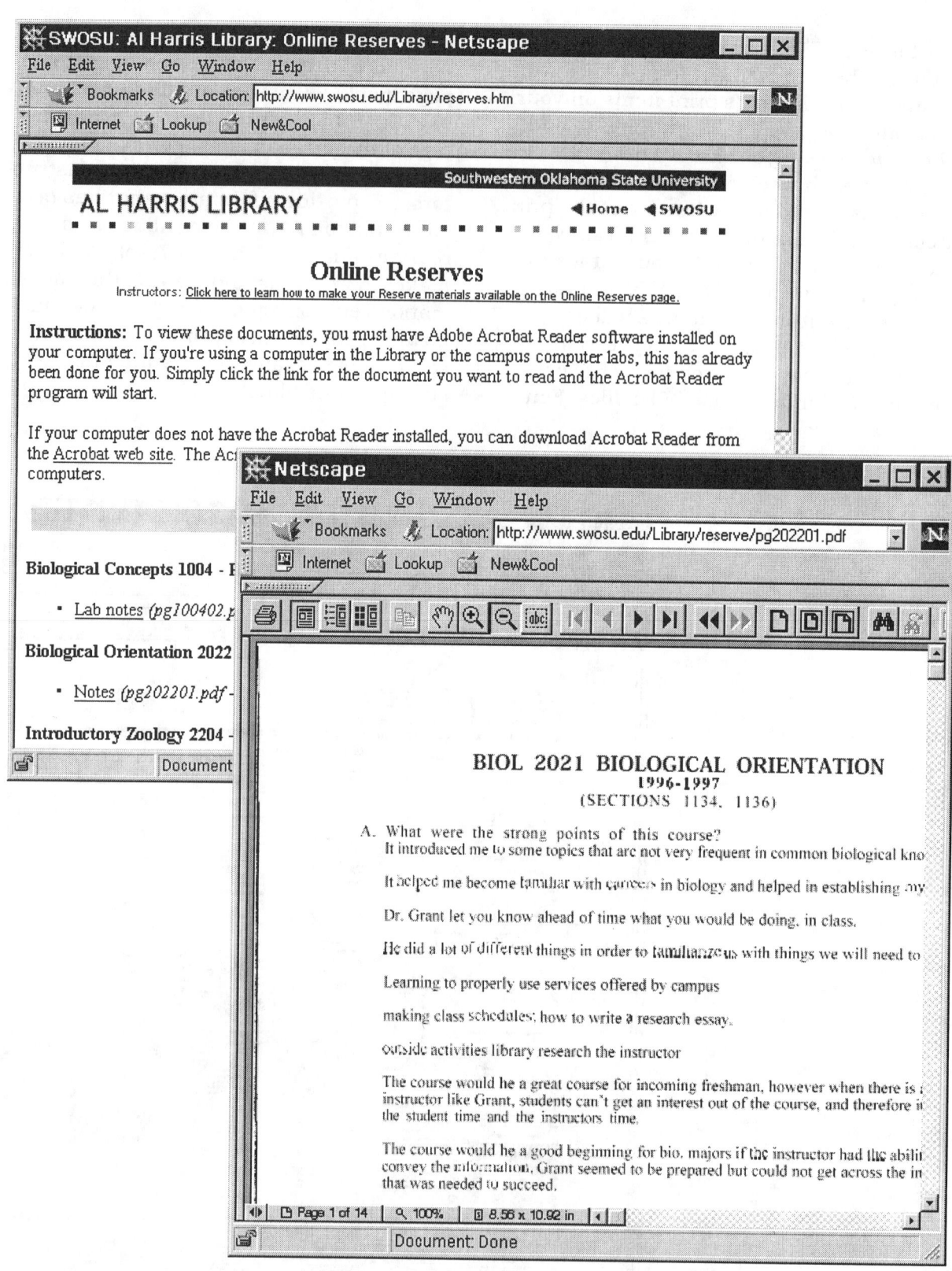

FIGURES 7.2a and 7.2b
Southwestern Oklahoma State University Library, Online Reserves;
http://www.swosu.edu/Library/reserves.htm

If your library publishes informational brochures for a particular audience, the use of PDF files might be a good way to put them online. This is what the University of Washington Health Sciences Libraries web site does with its "Books and Bytes" brochure, which is intended for the faculty and staff of the UW Health Sciences Center (Figure 7.3).

In order to create PDF files, you will need to purchase Adobe Acrobat software.

This can be a worthwhile investment if you are including or plan to include any of the informational items we have mentioned. Your users will need to use Adobe Acrobat Reader in order to view your PDF documents, but this reader is freely available and can be downloaded directly from the Adobe site (**http://www.adobe.com/**). This site also includes much support documentation and tips for using PDF files within your site.

FIGURE 7.3
University of Washington Health Sciences Libraries; http://www.hslib. washington.edu/hsl/bnb/

Shockwave and Flash

While Adobe Acrobat files are a very popular format for print-based information, Macromedia's Shockwave may be the preferred format for including multimedia in a web site. Shockwave files are created in Macromedia Director, a multimedia authoring application, and can be embedded within a web page, much like a standard image file. As with most non-HTML-based formats, a plug-in application is needed to play the Shockwave files in a browser window. The Shockwave player is free and available from the company's web site (**http://www.macromedia.com**). It is also included in the most recent versions of Netscape Navigator and Microsoft Internet Explorer.

Public libraries and school media centers have found that Shockwave multimedia files can be a way of interesting younger patrons in their web pages. Often multimedia can help children and other users visualize concepts in a fashion that cannot be accomplished with text. The Ohio Public Library Information Network, for example, has created an online instructional game that quizzes children about "Famous Ohioans," including astronauts, Indians, inventors, presidents, and women (Figure 7.4).

Other libraries, such as the Washington County Schools Online Media Center (**http://www.wcs.k12.tn.us/98/**), include links within their pages that lead students to entertaining Shockwave sites.

Macromedia Director, the application used to create Shockwave files, is fairly expensive, especially since it may seem that multimedia files serve little purpose beyond entertainment in a library web site. However, there is now another Macromedia application called Flash which is more affordable, and easier to use than Director. Flash can be used to create sophisticated animations and graphics in small files that can be downloaded quickly. Flash animations begin playing as soon as the first frame downloads, so there is no long wait for the entire file to download. Uses suggested for Flash include interactive buttons, advertising banners, navigation panels, logos, technical illustrations, and maps.

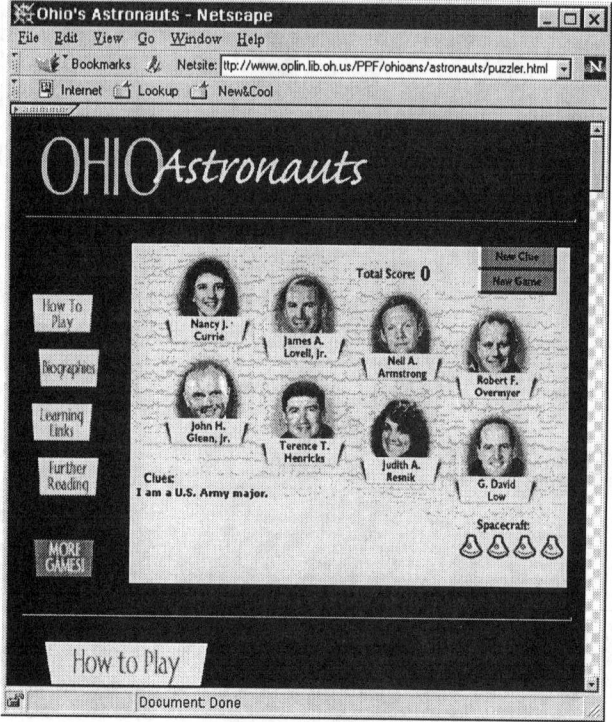

FIGURE 7.4
The Ohio Public Library Information Network, Famous Ohioans Shockwave game; http://www.oplin.lib.oh.us/PPF/ohioans/astronauts/puzzler.html

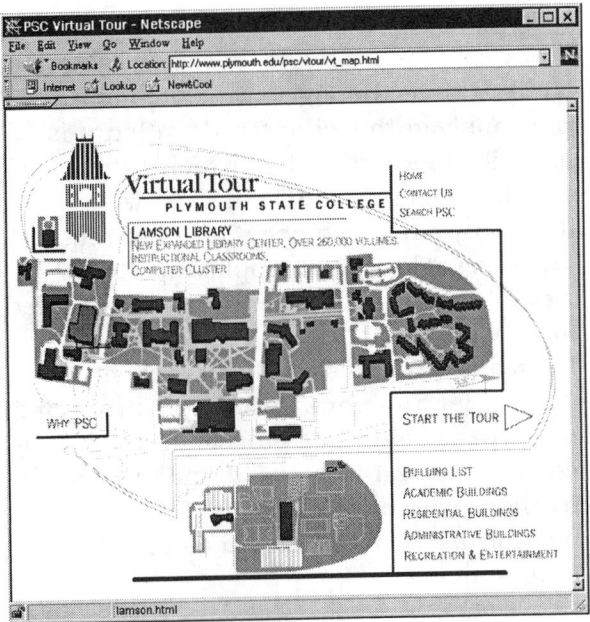

FIGURE 7.5
Plymouth State College Virtual Tour;
http://www.plymouth.edu/psc/vtour/vt_map.html

downloading at no charge from the Macromedia site. Users of Internet Explorer 3.0 and higher will have had this plug-in automatically installed with their browser.

RealAudio

RealAudio allows real-time audio to be played over the Web. Real-time audio is accomplished on individual machines by "streaming" from a server. This means that the audio files themselves are never copied onto an individual's machine, so there is no long download time. Users hear the audio at the same time as it is delivered from the originating machine. This technology is being used on many web sites to provide access to the audio of speeches, presentations, or other special events. Richmond Public Library and Eldredge Public Library are two libraries that have made public readings available on their web sites (Figures 7.7a and 7.7b).

The Plymouth State College web site is one that has used Flash for an interactive map. They have created a "Virtual Tour" of the campus that presents information based on the building or location you select. For example, passing your mouse over the Lawson Library on the college's campus map presents the information "Lawson Library, New Expanded Library Center, Over 260,000 Volumes, Instructional Classrooms, Computer Cluster." Relevant information for all the other buildings on campus is presented as your mouse moves on (Figure 7.5).

The Amarillo Public Library has created an interesting welcome page using a Flash file. This page is an animated file that moves into "Welcome to the Amarillo Public Library Web Site" and has text that alternates between "Let's Go" and "Enter Now" with the movement of the mouse cursor (Figure 7.6).

The Shockwave Flash player is needed to view Flash files, and it is available for

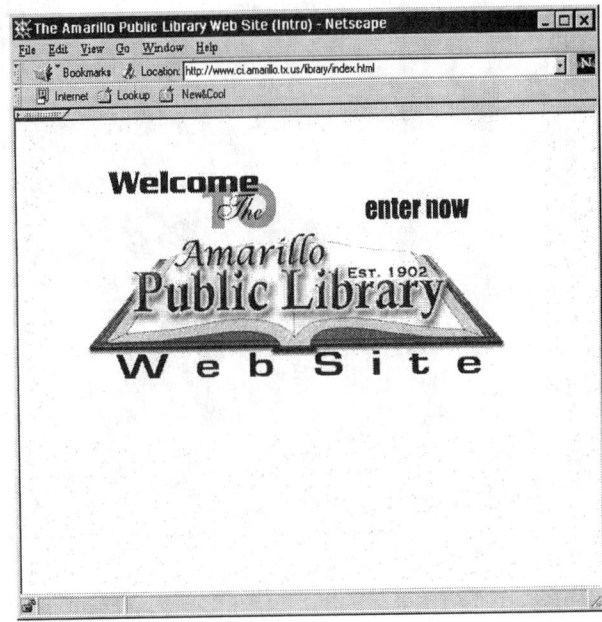

FIGURE 7.6
Amarillo Public Library;
http://www.ci.amarillo.tx.us/library/index.html

RealPublisher is the software needed for creating RealAudio files. It is extremely affordable and can be purchased directly from the RealAudio web site (**http://www.real.com/products/tools.html**). RealPublisher includes an HTML wizard which guides you through the steps of creating RealAudio and lets you preview results and make desired changes.

RealPlayer, which is free and can be downloaded from the web site, is needed to access the audio (**http://www.real.com/products/player/index.html**).

JavaScript

Unlike the technologies we have mentioned previously in this chapter, JavaScript is actually a form of coding which extends the capabilities of basic HTML. The use of JavaScript in a web page does not require any external software application to be viewed, but only browsers that are enabled for JavaScript (Internet Explorer and Netscape 3.0 and above) will present JavaScript functions. Although JavaScript is a type of computer programming, it is a coding that can be learned and employed by those who have mastered HTML. It is not just for use by professional computer programmers.

FIGURE 7.7a
Richmond Public Library, Young Adult Writing Contest winners reading aloud from their work; http://www.rpl.richmond.bc.ca/writers/YAWC/1997/

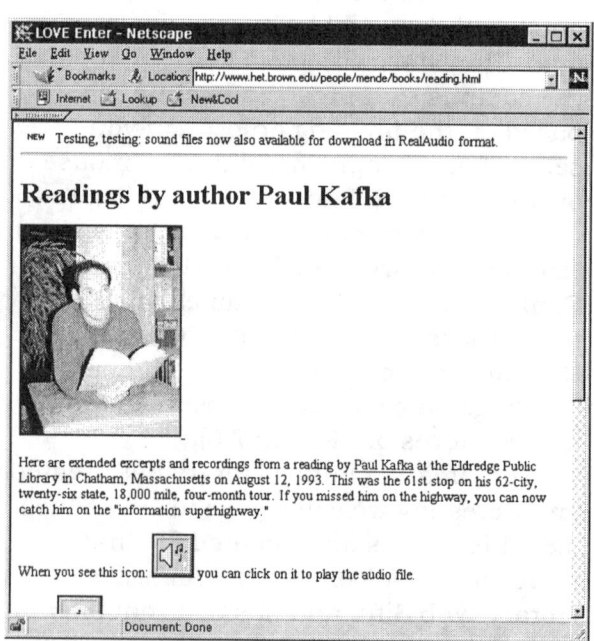

FIGURE 7.7b
A reading by Paul Kafka at the Eldredge Public Library in Chatham, Massachusetts; http://www.het.brown.edu/people/mende/books/reading.html

JavaScript is being used in many web sites to add interesting functions that could provide real service to library users. For example, JavaScript is currently being used in some library web sites to:

- Open pop-up windows with navigational buttons or instructions

- Provide context-sensitive or immediately responding menus on a page

- Create interactive navigational buttons

Pop-up windows. Pop-up windows are those that appear automatically when a page containing the relevant JavaScript coding is retrieved. For example, the Dallas Public Library uses JavaScript to alert users to its Internet Acceptable Use Policy. When users come to the first page of the Dallas Public Library HomePage, a window appears asking them to "OK" this policy. Users are not allowed to proceed further into the site until they have indicated their acceptance of this policy (Figure 7.8).

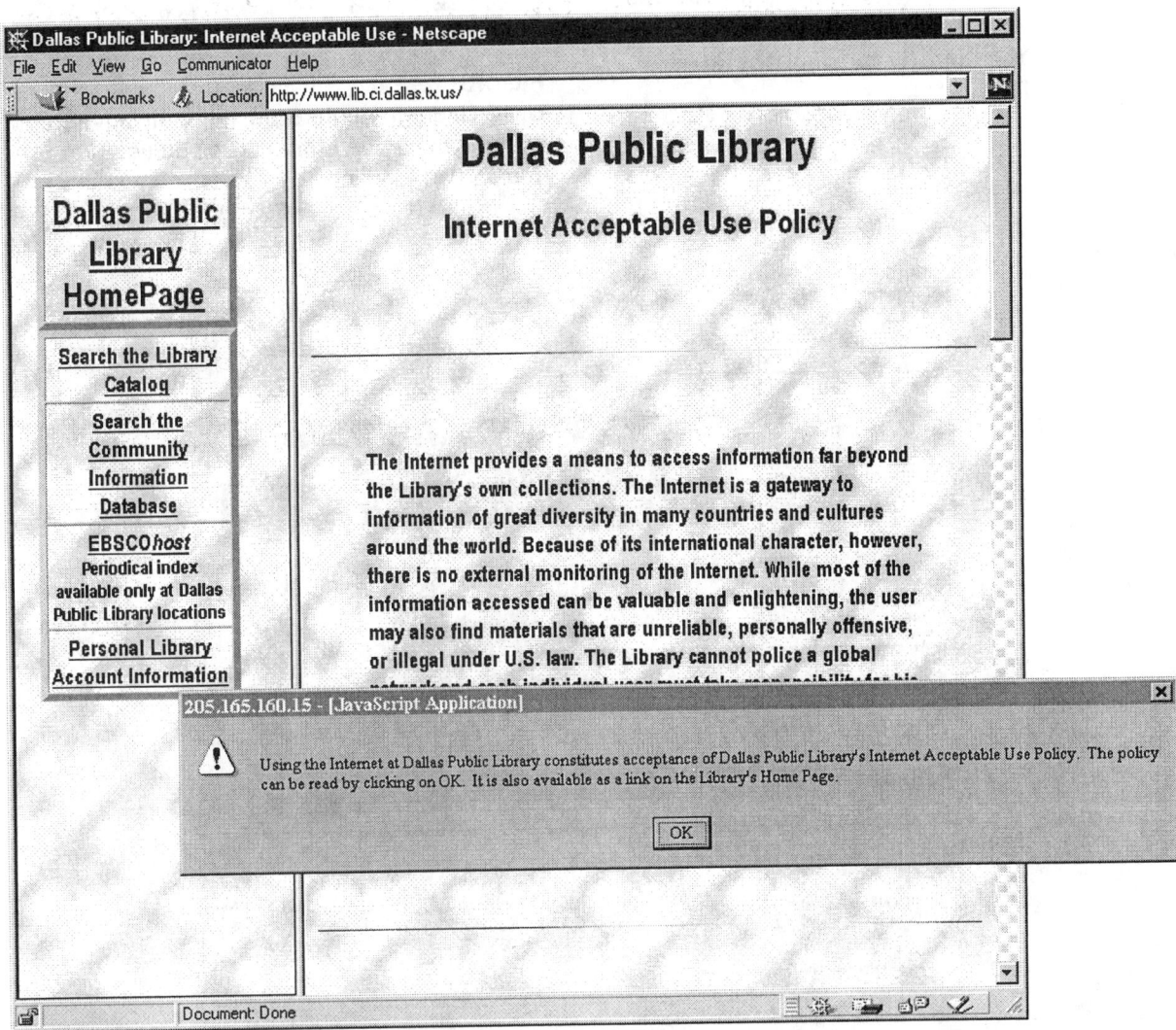

FIGURE 7.8
Dallas Public Library, Internet Acceptable Use Policy;
http://www.lib.ci.dallas.tx.us/

The Undergraduate Library at the University of Illinois at Urbana-Champaign uses a JavaScript-enabled window to open an index to its long *Undergraduate FAQ*. This separate index window can be placed next to the longer window with the FAQ so it can be used to help users navigate easily throughout the content of the page (Figure 7.9).

Menus. The Montevideo/Chippewa County Public Library uses JavaScript to provide a "Quick Links" menu to many local and Internet resources. Selecting an item within a Quick Links menu will move a user immediately to that resource. This makes the process of moving from the menus to a new resource slightly more automated (Figure 7.10).

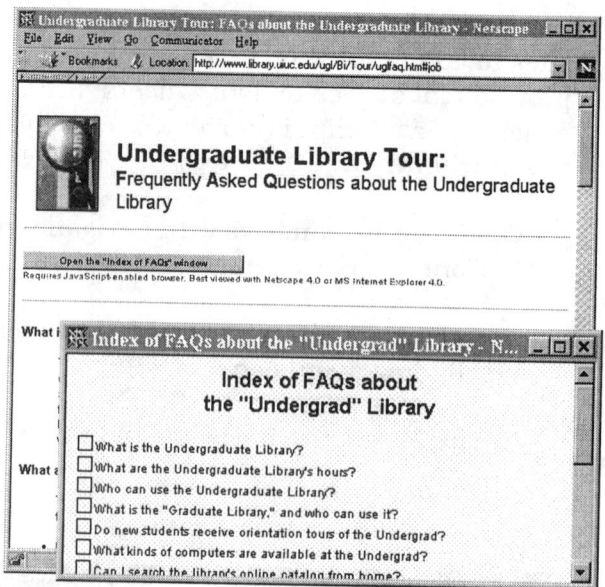

FIGURE 7.9
UIUC Undergraduate Library, pop-up JavaScript window; http://www.library.uiuc.edu/ugl/Bi/Tour/uglfaq.htm#job

FIGURE 7.10
Montevideo/Chippewa County Public Library, quick navigation; http://montelibrary.ml.org/

Interactive navigational buttons. The web pages of the Roseanne Barker Library & Media Center at Bishop Stang High School provide an example of using JavaScript to create interactive buttons. The navigational buttons become highlighted as the mouse cursor moves over them, and accompanying text appears on the page (Figure 7.11).

There are many JavaScript tutorials on the Web and in print, and many of these provide scripts for basic functions that you can cut and paste into your HTML documents. A good web resource to start with is an online article from Netscape World, entitled "Cut-and-Paste JavaScripts You Can Use Immediately"(**http://www. netscapeworld.com/netscapeworld/nw-11-1996/nw-11-javascript.html**).This article discusses some ways JavaScript is being used and provides some simple scripts that can be cut and pasted into your HTML documents.

As librarians endeavor to create web pages that reach their constantly expanding audience, these new technologies can play an important role in increasing the options libraries have for presenting information in more creative and flexible ways.

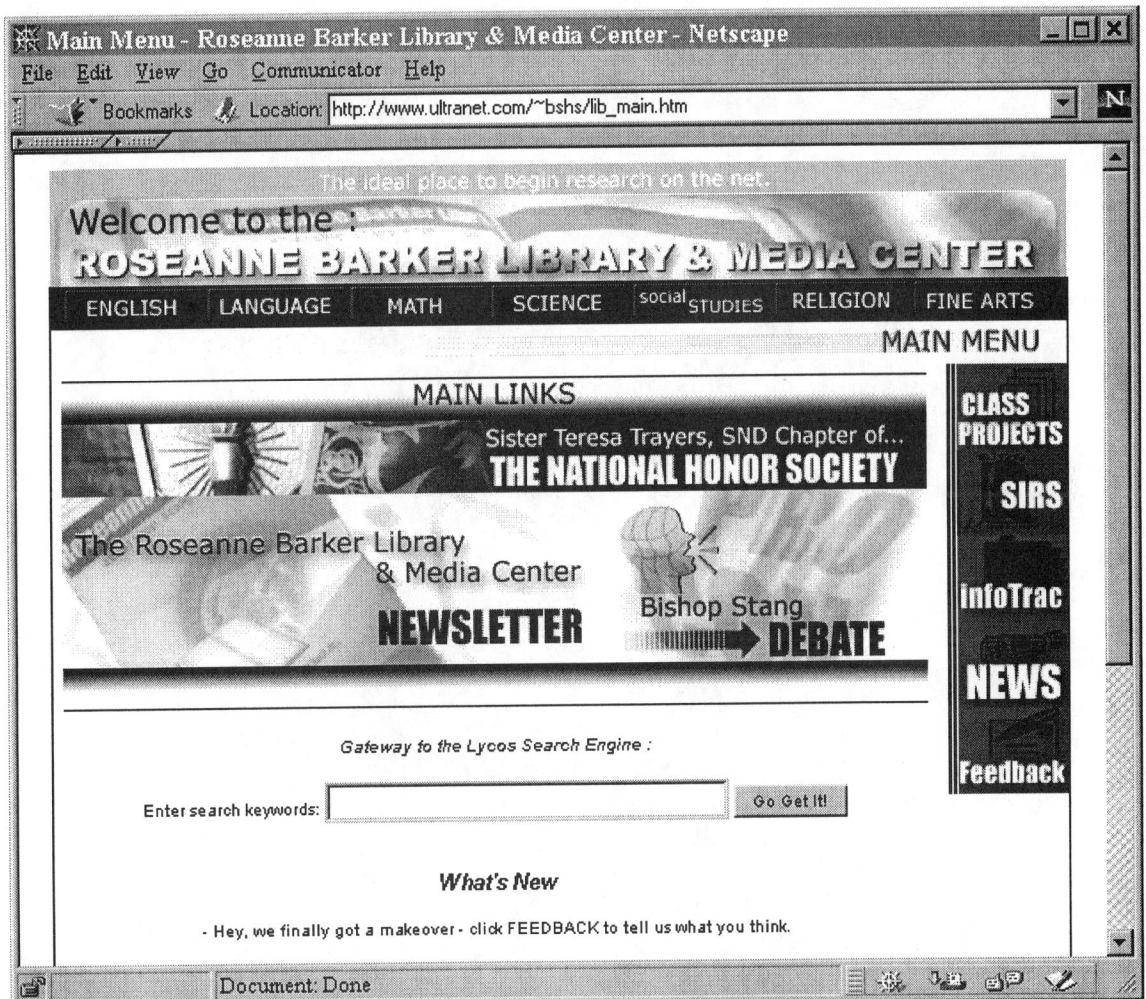

FIGURE 7.11
Roseanne Barker Library and Media Center;
http://www.ultranet.com/~bshs/lib_main.htm

APPENDIX

Online Resources

Presenting Content

Bibliography on Evaluating Internet Resources
http://refserver.lib.vt.edu/libinst/critTHINK.HTM

BUILDER.COM—"Put Your Database on the Web," by Bill Ho
http://www.builder.com/Programming/Databases/?st.bl.prog.feat

The DIG_REF Listserv
http://www.vrd.org/Dig_Ref/dig_ref.html

Electronic Reserves Clearinghouse: Links and Materials on the Web
http://www.cc.columbia.edu/~rosedale/

LibraryLand: Electronic Resources: Commercial Database Vendors
http://www.rcls.org/libland/elres/data.htm

Web4Lib Electronic Discussion
http://sunsite.berkeley.edu/Web4Lib/

The World-Wide Web Virtual Library: Electronic Journals
http://www.edoc.com/ejournal/

Accessibility

General Resources

Center for Applied Special Technology—Resources
http://www.cast.org/resources.htm

WebABLE!
http://www.webable.com/

HTML Validators

Bobby
http://www.cast.org/bobby/

W3C HTML Validation Service
http://validator.w3.org/

Assistive Technology

disABILITY Information and Resources—Adaptive Computer Products
http://www.eskimo.com/~jlubin/disabled/computers.htm

University of Toronto Information Commons Adaptive Technology Resource
Centre—Technical Glossary
http://www.utoronto.ca/atrc/tech/techgloss.html

Accessible Web Design

Trace Research & Development Center—Designing More Usable Web Sites
http://trace.wisc.edu/world/web/

WAI Reference List on Web Accessibility
http://www.w3.org/WAI/References/

Web Design Group—Accessibility
http://htmlhelp.com/design/accessibility/

Usability

Usability Professionals Associations: Resources
http://www.upassoc.org/html/resources.html

Heuristic Evaluation—useit.com (Jakob Nielsen)
http://www.useit.com/papers/heuristic/

Usable Web: Guide to Web Usability Resources
http://usableweb.com/

Web/Design/Usability—webreference.com - Netscape
http://www.webreference.com/design/usability.html

User Interface Engineering
http://world.std.com/~uieweb

Literature Review—User Interface Design
http://www.saskstar.sk.ca/doug/style/userinterface.html

HCI Resources: WWW-related issues
http://www.ida.liu.se/~miker/hci/www.html

Layout & Design

Color

lynda.com homegurrrl page
http://www.lynda.com/

Color, Value and Hue
http://char.txa.cornell.edu/zbs/webdocs/language/element/color/color.htm

A Palette of Background Colors with Options for Link and Text Colors
http://www.spunwebs.com/bgcolorf.html

The Greatest Color Utility/Hexadecimal-RGB Converter in the World!!!
http://www.insyncimaging.com/converter/

BUILDER.COM—Web Graphics—Great Tips from CNET Designers, Part 1;
Web-Safe Color Tips
http://www.cnet.com/Content/Builder/Graphics/CTips/index.html?ibd

Netscape World: The 216 Colors of the Web
http://www.netscapeworld.com/netscapeworld/nw-11-1996/
216_hexcodes.html

ColorCenter
http://www.hidaho.com/colorcenter/cc.html

ColorServe Java
http://www-students.biola.edu/~brian/csapplet.html

SUNY Morrisville LibraryLinks—RGB Color Codes
http://www.morrisville.edu/pages/library/reference/colorname.htmlx

Tables

The Table Sampler—Netscape
http://www.netscape.com/assist/net_sites/table_sample.html

Beginner's Guide to HTML—section on tables
http://www.ncsa.uiuc.edu/General/Internet/WWW/HTMLPrimerP3.html#TA

Something4Nothing Web Sites: Using Tables and Background Colors for Top-of-the-Line Web Sites
http://www.webdeveloper.com/categories/html/ html_something_4_nothing.html

Helpdesk
http://web.canlink.com/helpdesk/

Frames

The Art of Frames
http://www.spunwebs.com/frmtutor.html

HTML: The Definitive Guide: Chapter 10: Using Frames
http://www.ora.com/info/html/ch10.html

Sharky's Netscape Frames Tutorial
http://www.newbie.net/sharky/frames/menu.html

ViewSource: New Frames Tags (Netscape)
http://developer.netscape.com/news/viewsource/archive/ 11.95edelstein_frames.html

HTML Tag Reference: Frames and Framesets (Netscape)
http://developer.netscape.com/library/documentation/htmlguid/tags11.htm

Netscape's Frames: An Introduction
http://www.mcom.com/assist/net_sites/frames.html

Editors and Validators

Validators

Dr. HTML
http://www2.imagiware.com/RxHTML/

A Kinder, Gentler HTML Validator
http://ugweb.cs.ualberta.ca/~gerald/validate/

Dr. Watson, v2.05
http://www.addy.com/watson/

Web Site Garage: Tune Up Your Site for Free
http://www.WebSiteGarage.com/

Editors

Yahoo: HTML Editors
**http://www.yahoo.com/Computers_and_Internet/Software/Internet/
World_Wide_Web/HTML_Editors/**

Mag's Big List of HTML Editors
http://union.ncsa.uiuc.edu/HyperNews/get/www/html/editors.html

Text Editors

BBedit
http://www.barebones.com/

Homesite
http://www.dexnet.com/homesite.html

HTML Notepad
http://www.cranial.com/software/htmlnote/

Microsoft Internet Assistant
http://www.microsoft.com/msword/internet/ia/

WYSIWYG Editors

Dreamweaver
http://www.macromedia.com/software/dreamweaver/

Adobe PageMill 3.0
http://www.adobe.com/prodindex/pagemill/main.html

Claris Home Page
http://www.claris.com/products/claris/clarispage/clarispage.html

Web Statistics

Overview

BUILDER.COM, "Analyze Your Web Site Traffic," by Mariva H. Aviram
http://www.builder.com/Servers/Traffic/?st.bl.serv.feat

Web Developer, "Web Log Analysis: Who's Doing What, When?"
by Glenn Fleishman
**http://www.webdeveloper.com/categories/management/
management_log_analysis.html**

Software

wwwstat
http://www.ics.uci.edu/pub/websoft/wwwstat/

gwstat
http://dis.cs.umass.edu/stats/gwstat.html

New Technologies

Netscapeworld - Book Excerpt: WWW Plug-Ins Companion - October 1996
**http://www.netscapeworld.com/netscapeworld/nw-10-1996/
nw-10-pluginbook.html**

Adobe Acrobat
http://www.adobe.com/

Shockwave and Flash
http://www.macromedia.com/

RealAudio
http://www.real.com/

Macromedia ShockRave
http://shockrave.macromedia.com/

JavaScript

Sharky's JavaScript Answers
http://www.newbie.net/sharky/JavaScript/

Cut-and-Paste JavaScripts You Can Use Immediately
**http://www.netscapeworld.com/netscapeworld/nw-11-1996/
nw-11-javascript.html**

A Beginner's Guide to JavaScript
http://www.geocities.com/SiliconValley/Park/2554/links.html

developer.com—Directories—JavaScript
http://javascript.developer.com/features/js1.html

Index

Page numbers in italics refer to illustrations.

Sherry Piontek and **Kristen Garlock** are the user services coordinators for JSTOR, a not-for-profit organization which provides participating libraries with electronic access to the back issues of core scholarly journals in the humanities, social sciences, and sciences <http://www.jstor.org/>. In this position they provide support and training for JSTOR users, work on interface design, and evaluate new technologies for use in JSTOR. They are the coauthors of *Building the Service-Based Library Web Site: A Step-by-Step Guide to Design and Options* (ALA, 1996).

Sherry Piontek received her B.A. and her M.I.L.S. from the University of Michigan. Her previous Internet experience includes the creation of the original University of Michigan web pages, Internet training, and many articles and presentations on the World Wide Web and JSTOR.

Kristen Garlock received her B.A. from Albion College and her M.I.L.S. from the University of Michigan. She has conducted many workshops and presentations focusing on Internet navigation, HTML authoring, and library web site management, and is the author of several articles on Internet topics. Before joining JSTOR, she worked on the University of Michigan Gateway and the University of Michigan Library web site.